OPEN DOORS

Tarnya Coley

*To Uncle Alan
Thank you for your
support. See it. Anticipate it.
Plan it.
Tanya x
26.12.19*

Tarnya Coley

Open Doors

Authored by Tarnya Coley

©*copyright Tarnya Coley 2018*

Published by Marcia M Publishing House, West Bromwich, West Midlands the UNITED KINGDOM B71

All rights reserved 2018 Marcia M Publishing House

This book is sold subject to the conditions it is not, by way of trade or otherwise, lent, hired out or otherwise circulated in any form of binding or cover other than that in which it is published. No part of this publication may be reproduced, stored in a retrieval system or transmitted in any form or by any means (electronic, mechanical, photocopying, recording or otherwise) without prior written permission from the Author or Publisher.

MARCIA M
PUBLISHING HOUSE

Dedications

To the Coley family
To my husband and my two children who are always supportive

To my Mum and Dad for the encouraging words

Foreword by Sharon Amesu

In a world where our media channels are flooded with news stories of despair, hopelessness, fear and cynicism, there are desert level proportions of thirst for stories of hope, inspiration, opportunity and encouragement. Stories that remind us of what is possible when we choose to focus on what we have in our hands and not what may be amiss in our lives. When we get the opportunity to read these stories and listen to the heart of the storyteller, we must seize it and glean strength for our own personal journey. As we do so, we realise that the rich tapestry of our own lives is made up of the glimmers of hope that come from hearing how others have triumphed over tragedy, pushed through barriers and risen above brokenness.

Tarnya's book Open Doors offers us this opportunity. With a compelling sense of vulnerability, authenticity and courage, Tarnya allows us into her world and shares with us her heart, her hopes and her dreams. It is a privilege to join her on her journey. In many ways we get a picture of a full life with so many experiences to stir and move us to action. Yet we also get the sense that she is just part way through a life which is set for many more adventures, tales of triumph and Open Doors.

I have no doubt that there will be many who will read the words on the pages of this book and find the strength to fight another battle, sing another song and live another day. It is for these tales that we thank storytellers like Tarnya for sharing their story and playing her part in helping others to go through Open Doors.

Sharon Amesu- 'Leadership Coach, Women in Leadership Speaker.'

OPEN DOORS

Contents

Introduction 1
Chapter 1 Time to Face the World 3
Chapter 2 Leaving Home 17
Chapter 3 Destiny 25
Chapter 4 First Time Parents 31
Chapter 5 Open Door 38
Chapter 6 Home Sweet Home? 49
Chapter 7 Is it my Time to Go? 56
Chapter 8 Baby Boy 63
Chapter 9 Mission Completed 74
Chapter 10 Making an Impact 86
Chapter 11 Long Lost Families 107
Chapter 12 Keys to Leading a Motivated Life 120

Introduction

My life; my journey. Faced with rejection, low self-esteem, adversity and near-death experiences, I went on a journey of healing and, through that process I have found my true worth.

Life is a beautiful journey. I needed to change my perspective. I had to change the way I viewed situations.

This book is about my life, my journey and the many doors of opportunity that I was faced with. We come across many things when we are travelling on a journey. Disappointment, conflict, new opportunities, promotion and so on. We face many decisions and situations in life.

I call these decisions and situations **'DOORS'**.

'OPEN DOORS'.

What do we do when we are faced with a decision or situation, whether big or small?

Do we close the door and move on? Or do we face the situation or decision and walk through the door? What do we do when we don't get what we are looking for? Or the situation does not go the way we thought it would? Do we close the door and walk away and think, well, it wasn't meant to be? We have to go through a process first before we walk through that door.

I have had many opportunities presented throughout my life, and I still do. I have been blessed to have many people in my life that have shown me how to value life.

Throughout this book, there are seven legends that I speak of; past and present. They all have and, continue, to teach me tremendous lessons on my life's journey. Lessons of kindness, love, patience; how to be faithful and gentle.

Hero's come and go, but legends last forever- Bryant

Throughout my life, I have sometimes felt that I wanted to close the door on situations and walk away. Some of my life experiences were too painful, and rejection was the biggest obstacle that prevented me from advancing in my life. I allowed it to overtake my life and it changed my perception of how I viewed people. On reflection, YES, there was pain. YES, there was hurt. I had to walk through that door and learn how to deal with the anguish.

Come on a journey with me.

Chapter 1

Time to Face the World

"Your life is over."

"What have you done?"

"You're finished."

"Foster her."

Those words were playing over and over in my mum's head. These words plagued and haunted her.

It was a beautiful summer's day in June 1975. My mum was sixteen years old and pregnant. In love, so my mum thought, giddy-headed... now she's pregnant. "When am I going to tell my parents", she thought. She was frightened, terrified, alone and scared. She had to do this all by herself. This was real. It was true.

She was sixteen, and her boyfriend had left her. She left school with no qualifications, and her dad had told her to pack her bags and leave, so she did. My mum left home in the middle of the night and went to live with her first serious boyfriend. She told him everything that had happened, so he decided to take care of my mum. My mum lived with her boyfriend and his parents for a few months, but they then decided to move out and move into their own house. Life was on the up, but unfortunately, it wasn't to last. After a while, they broke up, and she went and lived with her sister.

Later down the line, my mum moved back home with her parents when I was three years old. If I was in my mum's shoes, I don't know how I would have been able to handle so much weight on my shoulders. I wonder if people thought nothing good will ever come from her. She felt lost, broken and distraught. She thought to herself, "I will amount to nothing."

"They were right."

"What am I going to do with my life?"

The baby's father was not around, and she had broken up with her boyfriend. Where was life going now?

The door to her life was closed, or so it seemed. Fast forward nine months and spring is in the air. The season has changed. She thought, "Maybe my life will change too". March 21st, 1976 came, and she welcomed her beautiful baby girl into the world!

Life will have its ups and downs, but what matters is how you deal with your circumstances. Your perspective will determine the outcome of life.

The boyfriend is now out of the picture. She thought, "I have to move on for my baby's sake".

"How am I going to let my baby grow up without a dad?"

"She will ask questions."

"What will I say?"

So young, with the world on her shoulders. My mum had to make a decision. A decision that she wasn't sure of what to expect, or what the outcome would be. "Am I doing the right thing?"

For me, growing up with my mum and nan was great. They were great role models, I couldn't have asked for more.

Let me start with my mum. She has taught me so many lessons and continues to this day. "You can achieve anything if you put your mind to it" my mum would say. My mum is a strong-minded and determined individual. Despite life's challenges, she strived to make her life have meaning and purpose. She left school without GCSE's. Back then, they were called O Levels. But in order to achieve, she had to start from the bottom.

"Never give up, what will you achieve if you quit?" I'm sure my mum faced many challenges as I was growing up. She never wanted to show it. She has a fighting spirit which I admire. She instilled in me the attitude to always try your best, which I now instil into my children. No matter the task, big or small, you must do your best.

My mum always treated people with respect. She treated people how she would like to be treated. "It doesn't matter how they treat you" she would say. "You have to see past that and see the good in everybody".

That was NOT an easy lesson to adhere to. "Why should I be kind to people when sometimes they did not treat me well?" I thought. There is a phrase that a friend always mentioned, when people were uncaring, "Kill people with kindness". That's what she used to say to me. People do not know what to do with themselves when you respond in that way. It makes them bewildered, and it is so true. Always treat people well. Your kindness will go a long way. Do not do things with an ulterior motive. But do it because you want to. You must have the right attitude.

My mum had no other option but to go to College. In order to achieve in life, she had to start with a plan and stick to it. There were no shortcuts to where my mother wanted to get to. There was no other way. She had dreams just like everybody else, and she was determined to go for it. She enjoys reading books and applying what she learns. My mum loves helping others to achieve their dreams and goals. She was a great believer in investing in other people. She also thought to herself, "If they can do it, I can too". It took my mum years to get the necessary qualifications she needed to qualify as a Social Worker. My mum longed to be a Social Worker, and she wanted to change the world. You have to have the end goal in mind which is important as this motivates you to reach your goals. However, she had to put things in place i to achieve it, and that is exactly what she did.

These *'things'* - I call them milestones. You cannot get from A to B without having a plan. This is my motto.

'Plan it. See it. Anticipate it' She worked out what she needed to do in order to reach her goal. She knew that it would not happen overnight. It would take sheer hard work, determination and perseverance. She was willing to work exceptionally hard to see her dream come true. So, my mum enrolled in a college course which she was so excited about. She had to work nights and studied during the day. This was a challenge, but she knew she could do it because she had that fight in her.

You MUST persevere even when things get burdensome. If you fail, because sometimes you will, pick yourself up, dust yourself off and continue the journey. You have two choices. You can either fall and stay there. Or, you can choose to learn from your failures and move forward. When you go through your different challenges, you can then encourage someone else who is going through a similar situation. You can encourage them and share what strategies you used to overcome the hardship.

There are different processes in life that we have to go through. If my mum was ever going to be a Social Worker, she would have to take the necessary actions in order to achieve a particular end. So, for you to achieve your dream, you have to go through a process.

It doesn't just happen like that. There is no magic potion or magic wand. You cannot go through life just saying what you want to accomplish. That WILL NOT produce results. It reminds me of a story I heard.

One day, a man wanted to have a shower, so he got up out of his bed and turned the shower on. He quickly got back into his bed. Then he wondered why he was not getting wet.

Simple analogy, but it gets the point across. You have to take steps, not just one step. You have to be continually doing something towards your goal. You must take one day at a time. Do not rush the process. Sometimes we want things done now; we want to see the change immediately. Things take time to develop and grow, so you have to be patient. Understand that you will get to where you want to go, but it is a gradual process. The results will not be imminent. Just take one day at a time.

I was growing up very quickly and was about to start High School. This is a very big step. I know this as I am in the process of preparing my son for High School. It is a massive transition. I was actually feeling OK starting a new school because my cousin was also starting with me. She was like my sister; we did everything together. We call each other sister-cousins. Her mum was my mum's only sister and was an incredible woman. There are different role models I have in my life. I call them "Legends".

THE DAY HAS ARRIVED

It is the dreaded Saturday. "Are you ready?" I shouted.

My cousin and I are going to my Gran and Grandad's house. I am old enough to get the bus on my own now as I am twelve years old.

Guess who is going to be there? You can't guess! My dad! I am seeing him for the first time, and I am unsure what to expect. Many things were going through my mind. What was great about my mum is that she never said a negative word about my dad. She thought that it was vitally important that I form my own opinion and I really respect her for that. This shows the character of a person. Despite what negative experience you go through, never allow your children to be exposed to any negative emotions you feel towards the other person. I believe this can have damaging effects. You have to work out your emotions and learn to let go and work situations through. Anger, bitterness and resentment can eat you up and can have long-lasting effects.

An hour later, we have arrived at my Grandparents' house. I recall that we would both sit on these wooden chairs and my dad would come into the living room and make meaningless conversations. Small talk; not much to say. He didn't know me, and I didn't know him. So, I guess sparking up conversation must have been difficult. To be honest, I felt that he didn't want to get to know me. He tried, I guess. Rejection is an awful thing to carry around with you. I carried this pain for years. I dealt with it the best way that I could. I just carried on with life as normal. Say nothing to no one and continue on with life.

For two years, we would do this dreaded journey nearly every Saturday. My mum thought it would be a good idea to meet and get to know my dad. She did not want me growing up not knowing who he was. Despite what happened between my mum and dad, she did not let that cloud her judgement. She did the honourable thing and gave me a choice to get to know him.

That is another quality of my mum which I admire; always thinking of others and doing the right thing. Regardless of how she felt, she did what she thought was right. I understand now why she made that decision. She didn't close the door to her past. She waited until the opportune time instead of making a rash decision. My mum did not act at the moment and was not led by her feelings. She stepped back and reflected, "What will be the right decision for my daughter?"

As we were sitting down, thoughts were running through my head. "Is it time to go home yet? How much longer now? I cannot keep on doing THIS. Speaking to this guy who clearly wasn't interested in me... I have nothing to say to him".

We were like strangers. Well, that is how I felt. Our relationship wasn't getting any better. I just found it strenuous and burdensome. I whispered to my cousin, "Are you ready to leave now?' She gave me that look, and I knew what it meant.

OPEN DOORS

Who knew that it would be the last time I would see him.

When I arrived home, I asked my mum, "Do I have to keep going to see him?"

I hoped she didn't think I was impolite. I was just saying how I felt. My mum knew who I was talking about. She was curious as to why I had asked that question. I looked up at my mum and told her why. She smiled and said, "You have made your choice. No, you don't have to if you don't want to". She allowed me to make my own decision. She didn't think it was right for her to make it for me.

There was a sigh of relief. No more sitting by the window waiting for him to show up. No more disappointments. No more broken promises. I felt liberated! It was like a burden had been raised. But I did wonder? Should I keep on trying and trying to build a relationship with him? Was I making the right decision? Should I close the door to this situation in my life?

Just as life was getting back into the rhyme, tragedy struck. The following year in 1991 my nan passed away. She was like my second mum. My mum and I lived with her until she passed away. I never thought she would die so young. She was only in her fifties. When Nan became sick, I remember the countless visitors knocking on our door. Every day after school my cousins and I use to go to Omco, our local supermarket and buy Nan Fox's mints (when they use to be in a packet and square in shape) and man-size tissues. They were her favourites, and this used to bring a smile to her face. It was the little things in life that meant a lot to our nan. She was loved by so many. I always thought she would get better and make a full recovery. However, she unexpectedly passed away. It was very hard for my mum and I. Even though it was difficult through this tragedy, my mum tried to remain strong for me.

When the news got out that night when Nan passed away, the street was congested with so many cars. People were bawling; grief-stricken. Some were standing there in disbelief. I couldn't go into the room where she was; I was fearful. She passed away at home in her bed. My close friend (now my step-sister) forced me to say my final goodbyes to my nan. I couldn't bring myself to do it at first. She insisted that I should go in. Eventually, I gathered up the courage to see her. She was lying peacefully; tranquil and still, with a smile on her face. That image has forever stayed with me. The pain of losing my nan was so immense.

My nan was another 'Legend' in my life. To this day, I recall stories to my children of what my nan use to teach me; the things she liked and disliked. An amazing woman, I wish my children and husband had had the opportunity to have met her because they would have loved her. Her life was a positive example to me. I can still remember the events leading up to her passing away. It feels like yesterday. I often think of my nan with fond memories. She had a great love for people, and many would share their problems with her. Not once would she disclose the information; she knew how to keep confidentiality. Many people would come to our house to spend countless hours with Nan. She was like a counsellor to her friends and loved ones. She would often give them sound advice and would never disclose anything that people shared. Those secrets went to the grave with her. This taught me how to be a loyal friend. A lesson from my nan's life was 'Trust'. This was the key to my nan's relationships. She knew the meaning of it and was faithful to the end.

I recall a close friend of the family saying, "Now that Mum has gone (that's what he called her), I will ALWAYS look after you and the family".

He was true to his word. He is my now my step-dad! Well... he wasn't until much later; the year 2000 to be exact. My step-dad is a true 'Legend'. Our relationship goes back to when I was a child. He has always been that father figure in my life, but I hadn't realised it.

Whilst I was growing up, my step-dad would give me advice which I did not always appreciate at the time. One of the pieces of advice I remember he gave me was always work hard and do not settle for anything less. I didn't think anything of it at the time. He always had great stories to tell. He had two children from a previous relationship. I was very close to them, and we remain close still to this day. He was fun to be around. I recall a game that he loved to play. It was called 'FAR AWAY'. Most weekends my step-dads two daughters, me and my cousin use to hang out together, and we were inseparable. So, the aim of the game is to hide as far away as possible in the house. Then he would have to come and find us. We played this game very frequently. We hid far away. "I know where I'll hide", I thought. "He will never find us", and he never did, as he had no intention to! Whilst we were hiding, he was sleeping. He would do this to us ALL the time! You would think we would have got the hang of the game by now. My step-dad just wanted to sleep, and we just wanted to play. When we get together, we always recall that game with tears streaming down our face with laughter.

My step-dad is such a great guy, and he takes great pleasure in helping others out. On snowy days, he would shovel the path for the elderly neighbours. He would deliver food parcels if people were housebound. He would go and visit the sick and be that listening ear to those that were in need of assistance.

All my step-dad wanted from all 'His girls' (that's what he would call us), was the best for us. He always encouraged us to work hard and achieve the best we can in life. In pursuing what we want, would always make sure we were happy. Never settle for mediocre, he would say. Strive for the top; believe in yourself; no one is going to do it for you.

Growing up without my biological father was OK as I had this great man in my life. I didn't always appreciate the encouragement though; as a child, I saw it as nagging. I guess that's how my children feel when I am trying to support and encourage them. You do not always appreciate it at the time, and I am so grateful that he continued to be there for me and give me the support I needed it.

When I got married, ironically in the same year as my mum, my biological father never came to the wedding. I guessed that he wouldn't come as we didn't know each other. My mum, being the good person that she is said that I needed to invite him. I gave her a look, only she knew what that look meant. She insisted that I do the right thing and invite him. I knew that he would never come, but I asked his parents to invite him to the wedding. My grandparents travelled up for the wedding, but he didn't want to come. I don't blame him, to be honest. It would have been a little awkward. My stepdad gave me away. That was such a beautiful moment! Such an unforgettable moment.

Death comes to us all. It is not for me to question and reason why people die young. I will hold on to the memories of my loving nan. The memories of the love she shared, her laughter and her big heart.

"How are we going to move on?"

We did everything together. I would come home from school and glimpse my mum crying. She missed her mum so much; so many happy memories. I guess that is all we could hold on to. That is what helped us both get through the difficult times. They say that time is a healer. I disagree. My thought is that you learn to cope with the tragedy. Time does not come into it. So painful,

I can still relive every moment of her passing away. She was an amazing woman. She's gone forever. It's just me and mum now.

My darling Nan

Gone but not forgotten.

Chapter 2

Leaving Home

Questions are going through my mind. I am a processor by nature. I like to think and contemplate, then think and contemplate some more. I don't like to make rash decisions. If I am asked for my opinion, which occasionally does happen, I will have to go away and think about it first. I have always been taught to think, before you speak and act. Always think before you do anything, as your actions can have detrimental effects on what you say and do.

Not only am I a processor but I also suffer from low self-esteem. It is very crippling; it dictates my every move. I hate it, but I don't know how to get rid of it. It has become attached to me like a bad habit. I have never told anyone, and I have learned how to dress it up. I learned how to become an actress; I was very good at it. I pretended that I was this confident and out-going individual, but inside I was a wreck. Those negative thoughts kept coming back to me; voices haunted me for years. I was a harsh self-critic and I had a habit of over thinking things; I was way too sensitive.

So, the thought of me wanting to be a teacher was absolutely absurd! It was actually laughable! I don't have the confidence to be a teacher. I thought I can't stand in front of a class and teach because the students will be judging my outward appearance. I may say something wrong; what if they ask me a question and I don't know the answer? No way, I can't! I was already talking myself out of becoming something that I wanted to be. But, I wanted to be able to impart knowledge to others and empower people. I wanted to be a part of people's journey and help them get somewhere in life. Deep down I knew I could do it, but I was scared; what if I don't succeed? I quickly had to stop myself. I had to believe that I could do it. This wasn't going to be easy, but I was determined to pursue my goal.

My mum is my greatest role model. I look at her life and what an example she is. Despite her rocky start in life, she had many doors of opportunity opened to her. She decided to go to night school, so she could get the qualifications needed to be a Social Worker. Working extremely hard wasn't easy. If there is anything I can tell you about my mum, she is NOT a quitter. Despite the obstacles, challenges, and the negative voices, she did not quit! As the saying goes, 'Quitter's never win, and winners never quit.'

My mum definitely had a winner's attitude!

Growing up, I was told I would amount to nothing. Not by my family, but by other people. I know! What a great encouragement. This is what started those negative voices. I was taught that the words you speak are very powerful. I learned a new phrase; 'Self-fulfilling prophecy.' Meaning, when you hear negativity over a long period of time; you become whatever has been said about you. That is what was happening to me. I was called hurtful names and always put down about the way I looked. You would expect these comments to be from children, but NO, these were hurtful remarks by adults! I started to believe the lies. This WAS like a self-fulfilling prophecy! I kept on hearing negatives words about myself, and I hated being me! I found fault with everything about me. This was not a good place to be.

On all my reports from school, it would read, '**SHE NEVER PARTICIPATES IN CLASS DISCUSSIONS**'. The teachers clearly thought that this was an issue and felt the need to keep bringing it up at every parents evening. So, guess what? In the whole time at school, I didn't participate in class discussions. That's a Self-fulfilling Prophecy right there!

"If I do nothing with my life, I will not make an impact in people's lives."

Well, that is quite obvious. I cannot continue to believe the lies that have been told to me over the years. A close friend of my mums would say to me, "Every morning when you wake up, look in the mirror and say, 'I AM BEAUTIFUL". "OK", I would reply, sheepishly.

"Keep saying it until you believe it!"

"Yeah, right", I thought, "There is NO way that I am doing that, you have got to be kidding?" I would look in the mirror, and the words could not leave my mouth.

This was an ongoing battle, a battle that I was determined to win. I was like a prisoner trapped inside a cell, but I was determined to escape.

I was broken and hurting from the name calling and rejection. As the saying goes, sticks and stones may break my bones, but names will never hurt. I am not sure who came up with saying but it is NOT true. Names do hurt, and it was having an effect on the way I viewed myself. Low self-esteem and lack of confidence soon crept in. Inside I was dying. I was like an imposter on the outside. How long can I keep up this masquerade? No one knew this was a cover-up. How was I going to get over the past and move forward? I had to start believing that I can and I will!

Life has its challenges. I couldn't stay in the place of negativity, and it would only make things worse. It was a downward spiral, being in that horrendous place which caused me to be overly suspicious of others. What are they saying about me? They are talking about me again. All these thoughts were going round and round inside my head. I could not get rid of the dreadful thoughts. They followed me constantly, haunting me every day.

I was still functioning but crippled inside. I so desperately needed to straighten the crooked mindset. The only way from the bottom is up. I had to make a decision. No more thinking negatively. I had to unlearn bad habits. No more warped thinking.

OPEN DOORS

I had to start believing in myself. I had to stop believing the lies, the negative and hurtful things other people had said to me. So, I started my journey of healing and made a decision to move forward. No more looking back. I will be free from the chains that used to bind my mind.

I am free to be me.

I believe I can.

I am unstoppable. How liberating!

When you know the truth, the truth **WILL** set you free.

Reflecting on my journey, I asked myself, why has it taken me so long to start making my dreams become a reality? The simple answer is timing. My mum always said me, there is nothing before its time. This is so true, I had to believe in myself before I could do anything else. If I didn't believe in me, who would?

If I was to sum up the word 'transformation' into *two* words, it would simply be PERMANENT CHANGE. I had to transform my mind, rethink my thoughts. I had years of damaged thinking to modify. The way I chose to speak to myself was having a negative impact on me. I had to transform the way I spoke. Transformation is a powerful word. Each day, I had to make a decision to make a transformation in my thinking. I needed to make lasting improvements. I had to transform the way I thought, spoke and acted. From this day forward, I chose to make a transformational change.

That's it! I've decided! I am going to leave home and move to a different city. Start afresh! Go to university. Make something of my life and make a difference! To tell you the truth, I had no other option but to leave home because the course I wanted to do was only being offered in Manchester.

Deep down I was anxious and petrified. I had never done anything on my own. I always had my cousin and friends around me; I hid behind them. This is now the time to stand on my own two feet and prove to others that I CAN make something of my life.

On reflection, I realised I shouldn't be doing this for others. I should be doing this for myself. I can do anything I put my mind to. But I was struggling to get rid of those negative voices. They were lingering in the background.

Is this a good idea? Should I move? What if I fail? What if, what if?

Then I thought "Yes, I am going to do it. I am not going to think about it anymore; I am just going to DO IT!

That's it, I made up my mind.

"Mum I'm leaving home. I have applied to university; I am going to become a teacher".

It was a bittersweet time. I didn't want to leave my mum all on her own. But this was not a choice that came very easy. I knew this was something I had to do. I knew my mum would be OK. She had her family around to support her.

"After your course has finished you can come back home", my mum said, with a smile.

"Yes, I can do the course, then come back home". That was the plan.

Well, I did it. I moved out and started on my journey to a new city to become a teacher.

This was going to be fantastic. This was an open door that I was excited about. I was going to meet new people; there were going to be new opportunities. Life was going to be great in this new city. Well, that's what I thought. I have to give this a go, I can't go back. What will people think? Here I go again, thinking about what other people think of me.

I moved into student accommodation. I was told it would be a great experience and something that would be lots of fun. It wasn't fun, and it was an experience that I would not forget as I hated it! I know it is a strong word but, yes, I HATED where I was living. From having my own space to sharing with strangers; this was not my idea of fun! I guess this experience was outside of my comfort zone and this was why I was extremely uncomfortable with this whole new experience.

After a year, the landlord decided that he was putting up the rent. I wouldn't be able to afford to pay those prices, I was stretched for money as it was. Working part-time, student loan and living expenses, I won't be able to continue living there. So, I moved out and moved to another student accommodation. It was a better house; better location, but that was about it. I quickly realised that student living was not for me. Just think, in another two years, I'll be moving back home, so I guess I can put up with it. That was my plan, but destiny was to take me on a different path.

Chapter 3

Destiny

"No, I'm not playing, I can't draw. Count me out", I said sheepishly.

"Yes, you are, you can be on my team", he replied.

I was at Mr and Mrs Coley's house for dinner. I didn't even know them.

Let me rewind.

I met these two nice ladies at the university. They were sisters. We got chatting about where I was from and what course I was doing. They were very chatty and friendly. They asked if I wanted to come over to their house for dinner? Well, their mum and dad's house for Sunday dinner. I accepted their kind invitation and was looking forward to meeting new people.

I didn't know a lot of people in this new city and making new friends did not come naturally to me. This was a great opportunity for me to mingle and step out of my own little world.

So, there I was at the Coley's house. The house was full of people laughing and having fun. The food smelt wonderful, I couldn't wait to eat. I remember the family were so welcoming and friendly. I thought they were such lovely people.

The family decided that we were all going to play a game after dinner. The only game that I liked playing was Scrabble. But this game was Pictionary. Arrrrgh!! I can NOT draw. I was paired up with a friendly looking guy. I later found out that this guy was the brother of the sister's. They didn't tell me they had a brother. Anyway, we were paired up for this game which I did NOT want to play. We didn't make it off the board! I told him that I couldn't draw. I have never laughed so much! He must have thought, "Why did I suggest pairing up with her?" I wanted to say, I told you so, but I didn't.

Who would have ever thought that we would we end up together. Destiny! That is what I call it. We have our plans, and we map things out. However, it does not always end up how we think it will.

Being new to the city, this kind young man showed me different key places. We quickly became friends, and after a few months, we started dating. He soon realised that he couldn't live without me and asked me to be his wife. We have now been married for eighteen years this year, 2018. I'm sure if you asked him, he would tell you a different story. The most important thing is we both realised that we were meant to be together. We were destined to be together.

One strange thing was, we would share stories of our past and would recall the same events. It became clear very quickly that when we were both younger, we used to go an event called Summer Camp.

At Summer Camp there were lots of great memories. But oddly enough, I never met him before, and he had certainly never met me. We both knew each other's friends, but... we did not know each other. We both laughed and looked at each and said, "We were not meant to meet each other until now!" The saying came back to my memory; nothing before its time.

We quickly got to know each other; we were similar in a lot of ways and different in lots of ways too, if that makes sense. My husband-to-be had a great personality, with charming boyish looks and an unforgettable laugh. He was everything I wasn't, and we completed each other. He would always pay me compliments which were so endearing of him. I admired his confidence and his outlook on life. He was bullied at school for being small, but that never bothered him. He always said small things come in great packages. He never allowed the bullies to get the better of him. He always fought back, until one day the tormentors stopped. What resilience! It's remarkable how we both had negative experiences, but we handled our situations differently. I was bullied as a child by adults and rejected by my biological father. However, I allowed that to affect me in more ways than one.

We were both young and in love! Excited about our new life together! The funny thing was, I had believed I was never getting married and never having children. But when you meet the ONE, it changes your whole way of thinking. New beginnings! I guess Manchester, the city where I was studying, was my home now. I didn't think I would settle in another city. I really missed my mum and my family and I still do. I had to think practically. My family were just a couple of hours away, so visiting them would not be an issue.

It wasn't a long engagement, and we got married on September 30th, 2000. It was an amazing day. We were surrounded by family and friends from far and wide. They came to witness this joyous day. The colour scheme was lilac and white, and the bridal party looked amazing. My Husband showed me the suit both he and the best man would be wearing. "That's different, but nice". On the wedding day, my husband-to-be turned up with a cane. I smiled and shook my head. Only HE would do that! That is his personality all over. He likes to be different and stand out from the crowd. As we are both musical, the evening celebration was a night of singing and live music. We surprised the guests by my husband rapping. He had written a wedding rap, and I sang the chorus. It was a huge hit with the guests! I was nervous to sing as I hadn't sung for years. But it was my wedding day, and I thought it would be a nice touch.

Who would have thought me and my mum would get married in the same year?

My mum got married in the May of 2000. She was no longer on her own. She too, found the ONE! She always promised herself that she would wait until I was grown up before she got married. She was true to her word. What a sacrifice!

We went to Spain; Lloret De Mar, for a ten-day honeymoon and it was fantastic! However, the method of transportation that we decided to choose wasn't. We did not have much money; we were both students at the time. We thought we would try and save some money and travel to Spain by COACH. We promised each other that we would NEVER do that again. It took us all day to get to our destination. Back then, you were allowed to smoke on public transport, and we were surrounded by smokers. By the time we arrived in Spain, we both had thumping headaches. Also, our legs were aching, and we were very exhausted. But that didn't stop us. The location looked picturesque. We checked in, got dressed and headed straight to the beach.

We discovered there were so many activities to do. However, whilst I was not very adventurous, he clearly was! He wanted to go on a boat and take part in paragliding. I DO NOT like water. He said, "I'm on my honeymoon, why not let's do it?" I sat in the boat and did not move, gripping onto the seat so tightly. He could not stop laughing; he thought it was hilarious! I DID not find it funny at the time. But ultimately, we had great fun, and we treasure those happy memories.

We started married life in a nice three bedroomed house, although we didn't own it. We were renting from a family member. We stayed there for a while and made it home. Then we decided to move to a one bedroomed apartment.. It was nice and cosy, and soon I realised that I was pregnant with our first child. It was January 2002, and I discovered I was three months pregnant.

Chapter 4

First Time Parents

It's a girl!
Born July 4th, 2002

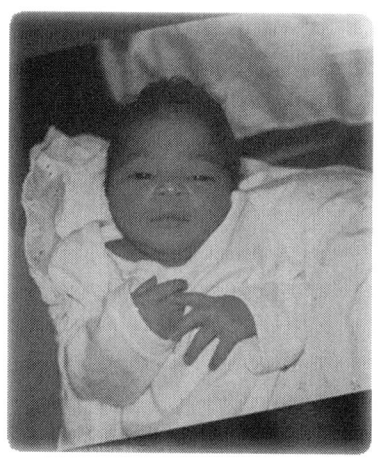

With a new one bedroomed apartment and a baby on the way! I was super excited! This new baby was going to be the first grandchild on both sides of the family. I was sick throughout the whole pregnancy; it was not a pleasant experience. My husband and I were excitedly getting ready for our new arrival. You could tell this was our first baby. We bought every baby gadget available. We went out and bought wipes, nappies, and toiletries. They were all stacked up in a box. You can never have too many I thought! The one bedroomed apartment was soon to be overtaken by baby necessities. What shall we name her? We both had so many different names for her, but we finally agreed on a name that we both liked.

She was due July 14th, 2002. My sister-in-law repeatedly would say, "This baby will be arriving on my birthday". I thought this was wishful thinking. However, nature decided that she was coming early. It was July 3rd. No way! My sister-in-law did say that the baby would be born on her birthday. I went to bed as usual, when in the middle of the night, I felt this urgent need to go to the bathroom. A gush of water came out! That's strange, I thought, because the water was clear.

I went back to bed, then needed the toilet again. The same thing happened. I was puzzled, what is going on? I went back to bed a second time. I felt a trickle of water run down my leg. I turned to my husband and said, "I think I have wet myself". Thinking back, what a ridiculous thing to say! My husband replied, "You probably have". He was tired, and I don't think he was aware of what he was saying.

Then it dawned on us! "Do you think the baby's coming?" No, I thought. She is not due for another 10 days. Let's phone the hospital and see what they say. I quickly got on the phone to the hospital, and I told them what has happened. You need to come in straight away, the nurse replied. My baby bag was packed, and off we went in our dark red Ford Escort Mark 4. My husband had not long passed his test. He kept saying that he wanted to pass his driving test before the baby arrives. He was true to his word. His Dad gave him his first car. What a nice gesture. We were very grateful as we could not afford to buy a car. All of our money was going on our new bundle of joy. When we arrived at the hospital, my husband called my mum to let her know that her granddaughter was on her way. My mum was super excited, got ready and came up on the train as she didn't fancy travelling in the car.

I was not worried about the labour, as I knew that was something I had to go through. Plus, I have a very high pain threshold. I kept saying to myself that thousands of women have gone through this before me, so I know I can do it. I arrived at the hospital, and the midwives were there waiting for me. They asked how I was feeling and did I think my waters had broken. I was feeling OK, but I was unsure if my waters had broken. I thought to myself "How can you NOT know if your waters have broken, you should know!"

The midwife was doing her routine checks, and she told me that I was only 1 centimetre dilated. What? Is that all? That means I have to stay in the hospital. The midwife stated that I would need to stay in the hospital as there could be a risk of infection. I was not impressed, to say the least.

Finally, my mum arrives; I was so pleased to see her. We laughed and shared jokes in the day room. I thought, if this is labour- it is going to be fine. Oh, I was definitely wrong. Suddenly a shooting pain in my stomach came out of nowhere, things got serious very quickly. No more laughing and joking, the baby is on its way. Oh my gosh!! I needed some pain relief, I was in so much agony, and I felt like I was going to die, and all they gave me was paracetamol. Really?

I looked at my mum, she's coming! This pain is intense. I called the midwife, she came over and "Everything is fine; you ARE in labour!" she said sarcastically. Then I felt the urge to push. No! She IS coming! And she is coming NOW! The midwife decided to check me over. To her surprise, 'oh' she shouted, "The baby is on its way".

I was in labour for twelve prolonged hours. Oh, the intensity of the pain! The midwife said excitedly, "I can see her head, come on just one more push, and she'll be out". By this time, I was exhausted; I couldn't push anymore. My legs were collapsing together. I was weak. I just couldn't push anymore. The nurse suggested that I walk around the bed. By this time exhaustion had set in and I said in a weak voice, "I can't remember how to walk". I was saying the most bizarre things. I put that down to the gas and air. My husband was there cheering me on "Come on, you can do this!" He prized my legs open and said, "Come on, push, we can see her hair." I recall saying, "Well pull her out by her hair then!" No book prepares you for this level of excruciating pain. I was watching the clock to see if I would go past midnight and sure enough, I did. I gave one more big push then she was out. Finally, after 12 long hours, my new baby girl had entered the world. She was born on my sister-in-law's birthday, July 4^{th,} Independence Day. "She's beautiful!" I said out loud. My husband and my mum were staring at the new arrival very intently. They put her straight into my arms, and instantly an overwhelming sense of love filled my heart. The midwife then cleaned her up and weighed her. She was a tiny thing; she weighed 5lb 13oz. I was desperate for the bathroom and was told by a student nurse to walk down the corridor. I tried to walk but I couldn't. Then she asked if I needed a wheelchair. I couldn't believe she was asking that question! Later in the day, we were both shown how to bathe her, change her nappy and how to ensure that the baby latches on to the breast. We couldn't believe it! We were parents to a gorgeous baby girl. After several days in the hospital, I was discharged to go home. What a relief! I did not want to stay in the hospital longer than necessary.

My mum stayed with us for a week, and it was fantastic! This was her first grandchild. In the proceeding weeks, the midwife paid me numerous visits to do her routine checks. She quickly discovered that the baby had moderate jaundice. She was only 4 days old, and I had to be re-admitted back to the hospital. I was not looking forward to staying in the hospital. I just wanted to stay home and enjoy my new baby. We arrived at the hospital with a letter from the nurse. We were seen immediately. The doctor sat us in a room to discuss what they were doing to get rid of jaundice. We were told that she needed to go into an incubator. She had to get treated to lower the high levels of bilirubin in her blood. She had to receive light therapy (phototherapy) and had to lay under a fluorescent lamp with her eyes covered. It was like a sunbed, and she had to wear something that resembled sunglasses too. Before they put her in the incubator, the nurse had to give her a cannular. My daughter was only 4 days old, but she was a fighter. She did not want the nurse giving her this needle, so she fought the nurses; she screamed and screamed. My baby became distressed, and the nurse was struggling to get the needle in. My daughter wriggled and wriggled, and her cries became more intense as she did not want this done.

"I'll take the baby; you go outside and have a break", my mother-in-law said. I think she could see that I was close to tears. It was horrible to see my daughter go through so much pain. After about fifteen minutes I came back, and the injection had been done. My mother-in-law hesitated at first, but then told me what happened. The nurse was still struggling to give the injection. She accidentally scratched my daughter with the needle on her leg. She became so distressed that she stopped breathing. My mother-in-law had to act quickly and breathe very rapidly in her face. My daughter started breathing again to the relief of my mother-in-law. My daughter now has an 11cm scar from where the nurse had scratched her with the needle.

I was enjoying my time at home with our new baby. We would often go for walks. I recall when my close friend called to ask if I wanted to go shopping. She also had a new baby; her baby was 5 months older. To this day, our daughters are 'Best Friends Forever' (BFFs). So, my friend and her new baby came around. We came up with this ludicrous idea to walk to the shopping precinct. It was a hot summer's day, and we thought it would be a great idea to take the babies out for a walk and get rid of the excess baby weight. We underestimated how long it would take us to walk to the centre. One hour later we arrived, hot and sweaty. We were so tired that we didn't want to do anything. Well, we were there now so we thought we may as well do something. We did some light shopping, walked around and did some window shopping. We then decided to walk back home, and it took us even longer to get back. We were both enjoying and embracing parenthood. The one thing my husband did not appreciate was the breast pads all over the house. He said it reminded him of coasters for some strange reason.

Chapter 5

Open Door

Time went by so quickly. Our daughter was now 11 months old, and I thought I need to start looking for a job. Every day I was looking in the newspaper searching for a job, but I couldn't find anything. I was buying the Manchester Evening News every Thursday; Jobs Day.

Then one day I came across a position, but it was for a teaching assistant. That was not the type of job I was looking for. I'm a qualified teacher; I didn't want to work as a teaching assistant. So, I didn't apply for the position. The search continued, and I was still looking for a teaching post. Several weeks went by and still no joy. It was Thursday again; Job Day in the Manchester Evening Newspaper. The same job was being advertised again for the teaching assistant post. I swallowed my pride and applied for the position. Within days I received a phone call that I had been shortlisted for the post. "Wow, I've been shortlisted, I can't believe it", I thought. I mentally prepared myself for the interview. I ensured I familiarised myself with the position and the organisation. I wasn't sure what type of questions they would ask, and I did plenty of homework.

The day had arrived for the interview. It was a cold, rainy and damp day. True Manchester weather! I didn't live too far from the school, so I decided to walk. I wasn't driving at the time, and there was no direct bus to take me there. When I arrived, I was asked to wait in one of the classrooms until I was called. So many questions were running through my head. I wonder if will I get the job? Will I like it? What type of children will I be working with? What if I don't get on with the staff? What questions will they ask? Stop! Stop!

Finally, my name was called. The interview was in two parts. For the first task, I had to read several scenarios relating to students in various situations. I had to write down what I would do in that position for each scenario. The task was a forty-five-minute activity, and I hoped I'd answered the questions correctly. I read over it again and added more information to the scenarios. Time was up now, and it was time for the dreaded interview. I took a deep breath and walked in with a smile. I was asked various types of questions, about myself, my experiences and my qualifications. Some questions I wasn't sure about, so I just decided to hazard a guess and thought what I would do if I was in that situation. That was the best way to approach it.

I have never been a teaching assistant; this was a new venture for me. Finally, the interview was over. They thanked me for coming and said they would contact me later that day and let me know whether I had been successful or not. We shook hands, and I thanked them for inviting me in for an interview. As I was walking home in the rain, I wondered if I had got the job. I wasn't confident that I had answered all the questions correctly.

I wasn't too sure, and I thought, I guess time will tell. At last, I arrived home, soaking wet. I quickly dried off and sat down to relax. I kept checking my phone to see if I had missed a call. It felt like a waiting game.

I heard the key in the door. "Wow, must be 3:30 already" and my husband was coming in from work. "So how did it go?' he asked. "It was ok", I replied. I told him about the activity that I had to do and the interview and the various questions that they asked me. I did my best; I thought if the job was meant to be I would get it. However, if I don't get it, a better job is out there for me. I had to stay focused and positive. My husband's positivity was rubbing off on me. My husband smiled and said, "You've got the job, I know you have."

The phone rang. It was 5pm. I couldn't believe they left it so late. By this time, I had given up, I thought the job wasn't mine. The lady on the other end of the phone apologised for calling at this time. She started to say something, but all I heard was the words 'CONGRATULATIONS!'. She thanked me again for coming and said it was a great interview and that I oozed confidence. I thought it was nice of her to say that. She said that she was looking forward to working with me and that she was going to be my boss. I thanked her and said I look forward to seeing her in September. I was overjoyed! "I've got a job!" We could not afford for me to stay at home as we needed two incomes. That was an open door of opportunity.

Unfortunately, and soon after, the reality of having to leave my little girl and go to work dawned on me. I knew it was going to be hard, but I had to do it. I had to go out and purchase new clothes for the new post, and I had no problem with that as I love to shop. September came around so quickly. My daughter's nursery place hadn't become available yet, and she was still on the waiting list. So, a childminder who was a friend of the family said that she would look after her until her place became available. This was great news as the childminder only lived across the road from where I was working. So, in the mornings I would drop her off at 8:15am. My daughter seemed happy to be left there. I guess it was time that she started interacting with other children more. I was heartbroken having to leave her as she was only 11 months old. I felt this overwhelming feeling of guilt.

I arrived at work in my new black suit. All staff had to wear suit blazers as it apparently gave off an air of professionalism. I had a tour around the school and was shown where my office would be. I was introduced to the staff, and they were extremely welcoming. I clearly remember being asked by one of the teaching staff, "So do you have any children?" "I have one. She is 11 months old". She then responded, "How can you leave your little baby and go to work? You should be at home with your child". I couldn't believe what I was hearing! I felt compelled to explain why I decided to go back to work. I didn't want people judging me. I didn't ponder on that too long as I didn't want to say something I would regret. I was the new person; I didn't want to make enemies. I thought, well that's her opinion, and she is entitled to it. I wasn't in the position to stay at home to look after our daughter until she started school. I felt myself having to justify why I chose to go back to work. Apart from that situation I had a good day. I was getting on well with the staff, children and teachers. Work started at 8:30am each morning and finished at 3pm. I couldn't believe we had to clock in and out every day! I thought they were joking. It felt like we were back in time. It was a gigantic machine on the wall, and you had to punch in your card on arrival and departure.

Days became weeks and weeks became months. I couldn't believe that I was in the organisation now for three months. My role was to assist challenging children or children with additional needs and support both them and the teachers in the classroom. I was getting used to the role, and I found great pleasure in supporting the children. I was helping them to make progress in their learning and in their behaviour. I remember setting up an initiative called "Self-Esteem". The clue is in the name. I built a team to support me in this new initiative. We would meet with year 7's who we thought would benefit from attending the classes.

At one particular lunchtime, I was called into an office. What have I done, I thought. I wonder what she wants to see me about. I was asked by my manager if I was enjoying the job. I told her that it was a great opportunity to work with children with challenging behaviour and help them in their education.

"Well", she said... and I wondered what was coming next.

She continued, "How do you feel about working in the 6th form as a teacher? A teaching position has come up, and I wondered if you would be interested". I couldn't believe it! I didn't have to think about it! "Yes! I would love to!" I replied. She went through the terms and conditions and the expectations of the post. She also discussed the pay increase. I couldn't believe that they had considered me for the teaching post. I had only been in the position for 3 months. Imagine if I hadn't applied for this post, I wouldn't have had the opportunity to teach in the sixth form, and this was a full-time teaching post. I was so grateful for this opportunity! I was looking forward to my new role.

It was 3 o'clock and time to clock out, pick up my daughter from the childminders and go home. My husband was already at home when we both arrived. I couldn't wait to tell him the good news! I excitedly told him what had happened this afternoon. He was so pleased for me! "That's great!" He said. "See, it all worked out in the end. I bet you are glad that you applied for that position". My husband is my biggest supporter. He is one of the reasons as to why I am writing this book. He always encourages me to move forward and not to settle for second best.

I stayed at the school for 7 years. I taught learners from Year 10 up to the 6th form. In that time, I had many opportunities to lead different initiatives within the school. One particular initiative that I was privileged to lead on was called 'Whalleyz Got Talent'. I oversaw the running of a charity event for the whole school. I had this great idea, but then I thought, "How I am going to go about it?"

First things first, I needed to advertise to the students the chance to take part in leading on a charity event. This initiative was called 'Learn to Lead'. This was about giving young people an opportunity to lead in some form of capacity and then they would be given feedback from me on how they can develop as young leaders. What a fantastic opportunity to have leadership input at such a young age!

This new initiative that the learners were a part of taught them some invaluable transferable skills. I will share this in twelve steps.

1. **Taking the lead.** It gave them the opportunity to lead from the front. If one of the students decided on a charity that they wanted to raise funds for, they had to take charge of how we would raise money.

2. **Set priorities.** By setting priorities; this allowed them to set priorities in order to achieve their goals.

3. **Be responsible.** It taught them how to take responsibility and not solely rely on the teacher.

4. **Ownership-** If this initiative was going to work, they would have to 'own' what they were doing. This would enable them to be proud of what they are a part of.

5. **'I believe I can' attitude.** When you believe you can do something, anything is possible. You will be able to accomplish much with positive self-talk.

6. **Solve problems.** When organising events, you will face challenges. However, being a leader helped them to look at the problem and see how they would overcome it. It made them think about what strategies they needed to put in place. Also, what were the recommendations needed if they were to do this event again.
7. **Make decisions.** This helped them to be bold and take action.
8. **Taking risks.** It is not just about taking risks and seeing what happens. It is about how to manage risk.
9. **Confidence building.** Putting on the various events inspired their confidence. Each event was successful. It was down to the learners to come together and lead in their various roles.
10. **Working as a team.** As you have heard the saying, there's no 'I' in team. It is about working collectively and playing to each other's strengths.
11. **Thinking strategically.** Whilst organising these different charity events, it was critical to think strategically. This is one of the top skills that you can develop as a leader.
12. **Effective communication.** This is a key element to being successful in your team. It is important when working with each other that you are careful in how you communicate. Most of our communication is displayed through our body language. Actions speak louder than words. The learners had to learn how to communicate in a respectful manner. They quickly realised that they did not all agree on

certain issues. They had to respect each other's opinions and come to an amicable decision.

At the first meeting, I was amazed as over sixty students turned up. This showed me that there was a need for this initiative and that they really wanted to get on board. Our first event was going to be raising money for the charity Children in Need. So, they came up with a plan. 'Let us put on a concert in the evening, showcasing the student's talent'. We could give prizes for first, second and third place. 'What a great idea!' The students were put into different groups. Some were in charge of the auditions. We decided to have the auditions for the different year groups, and this would be held at lunchtime and spread out over two weeks. There was so much interest that we had to employ extra staff to support the auditions!

The students were super excited about the up-and-coming event. I left the learners to build different teams for the various parts of the event. They were all in their power spot, and they made it happen with excellence. One team oversaw the sale of the appetisers for the event. They had to source the products, price them up and sell them on the night.

We had another team managing the ticket sales. They had to design and print the tickets. Also, they had to be at the door greeting the guests. We had stage managers, MCs and a clean-up team.

The learners gave me the task of asking three members of staff if they could be the judges on the night. The staff were very supportive and were willing to be a part of what the learners were putting on. The best part for me was hiring Pudsey Bear from the BBC organisation. Imagine trying to get Pudsey Bear in the back of a small KA car? It was hilarious! I managed to borrow him and some way or another he WAS going to fit! One of the students volunteered that they would dress up in the Pudsey outfit. This was a great surprise for the guests. There was a mass of children who were eagerly excited to take a picture with Pudsey, my daughter and her best friend included. Pudsey was a huge hit with the children. In fact, he was the highlight of the show!

The auditions were now over. The learners and I had a difficult task in witling down the artists as they were all brilliant. Finally, we managed to get the participants down to seven acts. There were various, different talents being showcased. We wanted the night to have a cultural variety, as this would represent the differences that we had in the school. There were dancers, singers, poets and much more. I took the bold step and opened the show singing the R Kelly song, 'I believe I can fly.' I received a standing ovation. There were a group of learners in the crowd that designed a gigantic banner saying 'We Love You'. How sweet of them!

The lead up to the event was electrifying. The students displayed the talent show posters in strategic places such as staffroom doors, notice boards and in the canteen area. It was also being advertised in different year group assemblies. The tickets sold out very quickly, and the students sold three hundred tickets. To our amazement, we raised £1000 for the charity. What an achievement! This was a great team effort. We all pulled together and worked to our strengths. It was a joy to see all the students from different backgrounds and age groups working together. This was a memorable moment! From time to time, I come across some of the students who played a part in this talent show. We always reminisce about the 'Lead to Lead' initiative.

For our other charitable events, the learners would get T-Shirts designed. The T-Shirts were different with various logos on the front, depending on the charity we were raising money for at the time. I would round up the sixth formers, and we would go to Piccadilly Gardens in Manchester city centre, with our T-Shirts and money buckets, raising money for the cause. It was great leading the charity events. The students were so creative on how we could raise money; from charity calendars to selling raffle tickets. We even made the Manchester Evening News! We were all elated!

My time at the school was coming to an end. I felt it was time to move on; move on to my next job. I like to call it my 'next assignment'. I was working at the organisation for seven years, and it was a great experience. There were many open doors, but it was time to move to pastures new.

Chapter 6

Home Sweet Home?

What drama! Why did we move here? This house has given us nothing but trouble. There was nothing sweet about this house! We decided to move as we needed more space. We had become homeowners, but we couldn't move into the new house straight away.

We had to live in the apartment and still pay rent which was more than the mortgage which we also had to start paying! I know, unbelievable! This was a very stressful time for both of us and financially stretching too.

What drama! What in our right minds made us move here? We were thinking "This house has given us nothing but trouble, turmoil and STRESS!" We finally moved into our house six months later, but there were so many things wrong with the house. Where do I start? There was wood rot, dry rot and woodworm, just to name a few. Bearing in mind, the timber and damp report had come back with no problems identified. The second floor was being held up by the floorboards due to the wood rot destroying the joists in the floor. The carpet was glued to the floor to hide the issues.

The builders quoted us £10,000 to fix the problems. At the time we could not afford it as we had other outgoings and commitments. All that was running through my head was, "Are you actually having a laugh?" We were totally ripped off by the person who sold us the house!

My husband and his dad decided to do some of the work themselves to save costs. They purchased the floorboards at a local DIY store. The sales assistant said the wood will be delivered the next day.

The next day a note was dropped through the door to say that wood had been delivered. My husband called the store as there was no wood in sight. The penny quickly dropped. The wood had been taken during the night without our permission. Welcome to the neighbourhood!

My father- in- law gave us a number for some builders who had done a fantastic job on his roof. 'Great! Let's use them'. They had quoted us £3,000 due to all the issues we had faced. He even commented on the fact that it was really bad of the person to sell us the house in this current condition and to hide the issues.

The builders arrived, and this was our first step to getting our home in order, or so I thought. We gave the builders half the money up front, so they could get the necessary equipment needed to get the job started. They put in a new window at the back downstairs and a window in one of the bedrooms. Also, they put in new floorboards downstairs, fixed the joist and put in new door frames. Two weeks into the job, the builder asked for the rest of the money to pay his workers as he was going on holiday and wanted to ensure that his workers get paid. We soon realised that the builder did not pay the workers and he was never to be seen again, and neither were his workers.

'This can't be happening!' The work was half completed and not finished to a satisfactory standard. I was having a pity party, and no one was invited. 'Why is this happening? Why did we buy this house? I'm living on a building site! This is no place for a baby to live!' I would like to say that I quickly snapped out of licking my wounds; but no, I hated the house. I would come home from work to a building site (which was our house). I felt like this for a while; all I was doing was focusing on me. I had to take my eyes off me and think about how to turn this negative into a positive.

My husband decided to do work on the house. It hit him really hard. He blamed himself that we were in this mess. He looked at me and said "I can't believe that I have got you into this mess. I didn't think that we would have so many problems. This was supposed to be a great experience for you and our baby. I never imagined that it would pan out like this!"

We were embarrassed to invite our friends over because of the present condition of the house. We would always apologise to friends about the way the house looks. 'No, we can't keep apologising'. Our house was a work in progress, and we owned this house. This was our project, so we decided we could take our time. We could decorate our house one room at a time.

My husband was committed to turning this situation around. This situation we found ourselves in could have turned out differently, but it was all about our mindset. We made a decision to look at our circumstances in a different light. I am a strong believer that when disappointment happens, you can stay in that situation or do something about it.

For about a year, my husband would come home from work each night and work on the house. He took up all the rotten floorboards and had to put in new floorboards. We became regular visitors to B&Q, and we had to spend money that we didn't have. He then had to re-do the work that the builders had done. They left the house worse than how we bought it! How was that possible?

So, we both decided to change how we viewed the house. This was our 'home', not our house. We were committed to seeing this project through. We spent ridiculous amounts of money on our new home, so that we could get it to how we wanted.

Then we received devastating news in the post. 'Your house is allocated for compulsory repurchase to build a £25 million school' our neighbour knocked on our door and asked, "Did you receive that letter about knocking our houses down?" We were astonished! "Really, knock all the houses down? NO, this is not serious. Compulsory repurchase? NO way! They cannot do that?"

After all we had been through! All the money we had spent; all the tears we had cried and the hard work my husband has put in. 'They are NOT taking our house!'

The neighbours rallied together and took the story to the papers as the council had just spent £300,000 modernising the surrounding streets including our house. It was taken to a decision at the Town Hall. The decision was overturned by the Town Hall to demolish our row of houses, but they were still going ahead to knock down the other side of the road. There were over 50 houses including local businesses. Once the court case was over, they resolved the matter by stating that they would keep our row of houses, but the council houses would have to go. I couldn't believe it! The council are going to knock down 120 homes and put the shop owners out of business just to regenerate the area. They were not interested in the people, or the people's livelihood. It was all about their investment and what they sought to gain. We were so glad that we got to keep our home. We could now move on and leave the past behind.

Excerpt from the Manchester Evening News

£300,000 on demolition homes 'a good investment.'

HOMES in Beswick have been targeted for demolition by regeneration chiefs only weeks after they were given a £300,000 face-lift.

A total of 98 houses on Sarah Street and Albert Street were sent letters advising them that their homes were being torn down to make room for an extension to a planned secondary school.

Angry residents have said they were not involved in any decision to demolish the houses and have been left devastated after originally being told their homes would be safe.

The letter said the extension of the 'state-of-the-art school', to accommodate 900 pupils, would be beneficial to the community and attract more families and the homes will have to go despite regeneration companies spending vast sums on new windows, roofs and gardens for the targeted houses.

In a letter responding to residents' concerns Tom Russell, chief executive of New East Manchester, said: "There has been full consultation with residents in Beswick in the last five years on wide-ranging plans to improve life for local families. Plans for a new high school have been integral to those improvements, and there is widespread public support for the school plans.

"Any residents affected by the development of the school are guaranteed a new home of comparable size and quality within the local area at a cost no greater than their current expenditure on housing."

Resident Brian Delaney, who has lived on the estate with his family for 12 years, has spent thousands of pounds on his house and has vowed to fight the regeneration company, New East Manchester, who is in charge of Beswick regeneration.

He said: "They don't understand that it's our homes they are taking away from us. We have put everything into them and if this goes through it would have been for nothing.

OPEN DOORS

"We were told four years ago that we could keep our existing mortgages. Two months ago they fixed up all the houses, and now they are bringing them down. It doesn't make sense.

"We have made these houses the way we want them after years, and we thought we'd be there for the rest of our lives."

The school is being built as part of the regeneration programme in east Manchester. Plans were extended when it was realised that more room would be needed to accommodate the extra people coming to the area.

John Connor, aged 79, has lived on Sarah Street with his wife Gladys, aged 80, for 45 years. He said: "We are devastated. The money they are offering us for our homes is not enough. We don't want to move."

Mr Delaney said he was adamant that no amount of money would compensate for losing his home. He said: "It doesn't matter how much money they offer. We can't accept it, and we will fight until the decision has been changed."

The school is planned for the years 2008/9.

https://www.manchestereveningnews.co.uk/news/local-news/300000-on-demolition-homes-a-good-1127435 (Assessed 23/01/18)

Chapter 7

Is it my Time to Go?

I remember as a child I always suffered with my tonsils. I frequently would get tonsillitis or bronchitis. I would even get this in my adult life. I made an appointment with the doctor as I was feeling unwell. He said I had two choices. "You can be on antibiotics for the rest of your life or have your tonsils taken out". I thought to myself, I really don't like taking medication, so I will have the operation.

The doctor told me about the implications of having my tonsils out as an adult. "Ok", I smiled and nodded. I wondered what could go wrong? At least I wouldn't have these problems anymore; having tonsillitis frequently. I was in and out of the hospital as I would have really bad episodes. I remember once when I was on the phone to a friend, we were chatting and laughing, then all of a sudden, the phone fell out of my hand and I noticed my hands and feet had turned grey and I could hardly speak! I was frantic at this point. What is happening? No one was at home. I heard the key in the door. It was my mum. She walked through the living room door, took one look at me and called the ambulance.

The ambulance came very quickly, and when I arrived at the hospital, I was seen immediately. The doctor looked at me and asked me what the problem was. I could hardly speak, and I pointed to my throat. He said 'Ok, open wide'. I could only open my mouth slightly. He said, "Open wider". I said, "I can't" in a muffled voice.

He tilted my head back and shone a light in my mouth.

"I just need to get something", he said and returned with an enormous needle. I have never seen a needle that long. I was petrified. What on earth is he going to do with that?

He saw my panic-stricken face and reassured me that it was going to be ok. "All I am going to do is pop the needle in your mouth. There is a large cyst full of pus and blood at the back of your throat; also, your tonsils are inflamed. It won't hurt" he reassured me.

Oh, my goodness! As he took this long needle and put it in my throat, he popped the cyst. I screamed as the pain was excruciating. Blood and puss gushed out of my mouth. He gave me a drink of water rinsed my mouth out. He said, "I told you it wouldn't hurt, it wasn't that bad was it?" I took one look at him. I think he knew what that look meant! The pain was awful. But I was grateful that the cyst had gone. "Right Mum, we can go home". The doctor quickly replied, "No, you can't. They are admitting you to hospital. We are going to put you on a course of antibiotics, you are dehydrated. You cannot go home in that condition".

I was mortified! I hate hospitals. I looked at my mum as if she could rescue me. I gave her the 'puppy eyes' look. It didn't work.

"If the doctor says you need to stay, you need to stay", she said in a motherly voice.

Thanks, Mum, I thought.

I stayed in the hospital for a week. The doctor said I couldn't go home until I started eating and drinking, but I had lost my appetite. I thought I don't want to be in here longer than necessary. So, I forced myself to eat and drink. The nurses were monitoring me, writing down everything I ate and drank. The nurses were monitoring my progress to see if I was well enough to go home. The doctor checked my tonsils and said he was happy to discharge me. What a relief!

The thought of having my tonsils removed as an adult was great news. I didn't want to go through that pain and agony anymore. The doctor said I would receive a letter adding a date for my tonsils to be removed.

I was actually looking forward having my tonsils out. I knew I didn't have to go through the pain that I have lived with all my life. I informed work about my admission and that I would need one week off. They wished me all the best and said let us know how you get on.

The day had arrived, and my husband accompanied me to the hospital. The nurse went through the usual procedures; going through the family history and asking lots of questions. Then I had to sit and wait to be called. You know what it's like in hospitals sometimes. "I hope I'm not sitting here for ages". I waited patiently as I knew my time was coming soon. On the other hand, my husband was getting agitated saying "This is taking a long time".

They called my name out next. I was prepped and ready to go down to theatre. I had to sign a consent form as I was going under local anaesthetic. They looked at my husband and said she won't be long. As I was wheeled down to the theatre, they were asking me a series of questions. I thought they are just waiting for me to go off to sleep. They were very nice, and that was part of their job, to make me feel more comfortable and at ease. My husband waited and waited by my bedside until I had come out of the theatre. Hours later I was wheeled back to my hospital bed. My husband greeted me with a nice smile. He asked the staff. "Did everything go ok?'. "Yes", they replied quickly.

Something didn't feel right. I felt as if I was dying. I was drifting away. I gripped my husband's hand in panic and said "Something's not right. I don't feel good. I'm going".

He said "You're ok, you have just had an operation. You will feel better soon".

Then I started to vomit blood. Blood was pouring out of my mouth like a gush of water. I could feel the blood trickling down the back of my throat. Clumps of blood were coming out of my mouth, and my body went limp.

My husband called the nurses; the staff had to support me to sit up. With the look on their faces, I could tell that's something wasn't right. I could see they tried not to panic and started talking in code.

What's going on? It felt like an episode of Holby City. There were doctors and nurses rushing around. They drew the curtains, and I thought it was curtains for me!

They said to my husband, "Actually, we had complications taking the left tonsil out. The right tonsil was larger than usual. She will have to go back in for surgery. As this is an emergency, you will have to sign the papers". I was rushed back into theatre for the second time. When I came back out my husband was relieved!

The second time around, the procedure was longer than the first; approximately three hours. My husband at this point didn't care about how long the operation was. He was relieved his wife was ok. I could hardly speak and move. I was the worst for wear. I was talking very muffled as if a ball of wool was down my throat. To swallow was very painful. I was given ice cream to soothe my throat. I wasn't up eating and drinking as I just wanted to lie down.

My friend from work called to ask how the operation went. I could hardly speak; she asked if she could come up and visit me. I told her that my hair is a mess and that I look awful. She didn't care about that, "I'll be there after work".

When she arrived, she looked at me and said, "What's happened? I thought you just had your tonsils out!" That indicated to me that I looked dreadful. We laughed (well I couldn't move my shoulders up and down). She was sharing with me what had been happening at work. I was so grateful for her visit. Even though we had now both left the place we were working, we kept in touch. She now has a PhD in Educational Psychology and lives in the leafy suburbs of Derbyshire.

When I arrived home, my parents called me. They quickly drove down to see me. We decided it would be best for me to go back to my parents' house to look after me. I was on a lot of medication, and I could hardly do anything for myself. My daughter was about two at the time, and I couldn't look after her. I was so weak, I couldn't pick her up. She would often tap me and say "Mummy, not talking." She could see that something was different about me. I could only smile and look at her and say, "Mummy's ok", in a distorted voice.

I had to call into work and let them know what had happened. They were in shock!

It wasn't until much later that I was able to go back to work. A simple procedure turned out to be a nightmare.

Isn't it great when you have a support network around you? My parents nursed me back to health. They looked after me and my daughter and took great pride in doing so. You are probably thinking 'Well, they are your parents'. But not everyone has a supportive family around them. I do not take anything for granted. They didn't have to do what they did, but they chose to. The support and love that they showed me aided a quick recovery.

One simple word comes to mind ... LOVE. The greatest thing in the world. Always appreciate what you have. Do not wait until it is gone.

Chapter 8

Baby Boy

I had a miscarriage previously. So, finding out that I was pregnant again was out of this world! Just like the first pregnancy, I was sick for the full duration of the pregnancy. I was still working at the school and couldn't wait to tell them the good news. I decided to wait until I had the three-month scan.

When I was pregnant previously, I had told everyone, but then I had a miscarriage. People were coming up to me asking how the pregnancy was going. Telling them that I had a miscarriage was very painful. So, I thought this time, I will not say a word.

My husband took the day off work to accompany me to the hospital. "What do you think we are having?" he asked. I sarcastically replied, "Either a boy, or a girl!" We arrived at the hospital and were quickly called in. 'Would you like to know what you are having?' We both replied, 'Yes'. 'Congratulations! You are having a boy' was the response.

We were over the moon!

Just like my first pregnancy, I was sick for the whole nine months. But let me bypass the nine months of pregnancy; my baby was born with a tracheo-oesophageal fistula; fistula for short. This is where all the hospital visits started.

When my baby was born, he was sick, but we just didn't know what was wrong with him. We would take him to the hospital, and the medical staff would check him over, but they couldn't find anything. Who was to know that this is going to be one of many trips we would take because unfortunately, our baby was sick for a very long time. The pain for us as parents was intense and my husband and I just didn't know what was wrong. But we knew that there was something not right. Still, the doctors couldn't find anything specific. There were many suggestions from the professionals as to what the problem could be;

"He has asthma."
"He has breathing problems."
"Mum, you're not feeding him properly."
Let me take you back to the beginning of this journey.

My son was born ten days early. Shortly after he was born, I was breastfeeding him, and he started choking. My mum called the ambulance. I was panic-stricken, but I didn't want to show it; my mum is just the same, we're just like each other. We went to the hospital, and they told me that he is just choking because my milk ducts were flowing too fast. They gave me a triangular pillow to prop him up. Well, I hadn't ever heard such a ridiculous thing! I was sure my baby wasn't turning blue because of my milk ducts! They checked him over and sent us home.

I phoned my husband and told him what had happened and the medical staff's verdict. He said "That's strange! Why would they think it is your milk ducts?" So, the midwife came around and gave me a support pillow, so my baby could be supported in the correct way, and the milk would be flowing more slowly. But that didn't help either, yet they told me just to keep on trying. Every now and again he would have a cough, and my friend described it as a grandad cough. The baby was growing older; he was now six months old we started introducing foods to him. However, he could not manage the foods, and he kept choking on the food. We tried giving him a bottle which made it even worse. He was choking on the bottle and bubbles would flow out of his mouth. It reminded me of when you run a bath and put an excessive amount of bubble bath in there, and the bubbles start foaming. I had NEVER seen that before! What do you do when the midwives can't help, and the hospital is not helping? I decided to make an appointment with our GP. I told the doctor what was happening, and they said they would refer us and the baby to the hospital. We felt that we were being pushed from pillar to post. This ordeal lasted for sixteen months.

One day, my son took a turn for the worse. He stopped eating and drinking. This was during a half-term holiday. My husband took him to the hospital, and they kept him in overnight. He was checked by the doctors, and they still couldn't find anything wrong. Again, they sent him home. I was surprised to see my husband home so quickly. He said that they didn't know what was wrong with him.

He was getting worse. I thought I would take a chance and take him to the hospital. They checked him over as usual, and they asked me to wait whilst they discussed this case. They drew the curtains, and I heard them say in a whisper, "We just don't know what is wrong with this child, send Mum home". They drew back the curtains, and they looked at me and said, "We can't see what the matter is". I went home feeling very frustrated. My husband and I just did not know what to do.

My mother-in-law said to me "You must make an appointment with the doctor and tell them everything". So, the next day, I did just that. They took one look at him and called the ambulance. They wrote a note and sent me on my way.

I told my mother-in-law what was happening, and she said I was not to leave the hospital until I got some answers. I arrived at the hospital, distressed, broken and confused. I knew there was something wrong, but what exactly was the problem?

This kind doctor called me over and told me she would be checking our son over. She took one look at him and noted there was something definitely wrong. She said, "I have a son exactly the same age as yours, and your son seems to be underweight and looks very ill.

I know what I will do, I will carry out a dye test. Your son will have to drink the dye, and we will have a look on the X-ray to see what happens when he drinks it".

OPEN DOORS

I watched in anticipation as to what was going to happen. To our surprise, the dye was going into his lungs.

The doctor proceeded to inform me. "I've found the problem. When your son eats and drinks, some of the food is going into his lungs. This is what is causing the bubbles to come out of his mouth. Therefore, he is underweight and not developing as he should. This is the reason why he has bow legs, it is because of malnutrition".

She continued, "I will have to discuss this matter with the other doctors to see what we are going to do next".

I was so relieved that they had found what it was. It wasn't my milk ducts, or asthma or me not feeding him correctly. He had a hole in his lung!

We were both admitted to the hospital. By this time three days have passed, and he hadn't eaten anything. They decided to put my son on a drip to help him be hydrated. I sat and waited in the hospital for the doctors to come back with a decision as to what they were going to do.

The doctors came back looking very serious. "This is a delicate matter. We are going to refer you to St Mary's. We will have to perform surgery to rectify the problem". I thought this was fantastic news. Finally, something was going to be done about it.

They said, "When your son wakes up we will take you by ambulance to St. Mary's".

We arrived at St Mary's hospital, and the staff were very friendly. My husband met me at the hospital as he didn't work too far from there. They settled us down in a hospital ward very quickly. They had to put another drip on my son. Each time they had to do this, he cried hysterically. He had been prodded and poked so many times in the last sixteen months. It was painful to watch as I knew it was distressing him.

I asked the nurse if she knew when the operation would take place. She replied, "I will ask the doctor and come back to you; actually, I will ask him to come to discuss the matter with you and your husband".

The doctor was doing his rounds, and finally, the medical staff came to us. They began to tell us what was going to happen. "The surgery will be performed within the next week as the doctor who is going to perform is away on business now". They saw our faces drop because we thought he would have surgery immediately. The doctor quickly added, "This particular surgeon is the BEST in the country. He is the best person to carry this out particular surgery. Are you prepared to wait?"

We both agreed that this was the best option. We felt so blessed that our son was receiving the best care in the hospital!

Days felt like months but finally, the day of the operation was here.

We sat in the doctor's office as we discussed the procedure. "Can I be honest with you both?" he asked. We looked at each other with a puzzled look. "Of course". He continued, "The truth is your son is lucky to be alive. I don't understand how he is still living. He is very poorly. The best way to perform this surgery was to make an incision to cut his neck and tie the tubes so no more food will be going into his lungs. This is a very delicate procedure. Once this has been carried out over the years, it can revert back. However, I feel this will be a successful operation. This is a very rare condition, and the operation will take up to four hours. Once we have carried out the procedure, we will call you. Please be prepared as he will have lots of tubes sticking out and he will be on a life support machine. This will be to stabilise him. He will be in the hospital for approximately six weeks. Mum, you can stay at the hospital with him. There are rooms upstairs where you can sleep. Have you got any questions?"

We were struck with silence. We couldn't believe our little boy was going to go through all this.

It was time for the surgery. I walked our son down to the theatre, kissed him on his cheek goodbye and said, "See you later, son".

The doctor turned to me and said, "Mum, he's going to be ok, he's in good hands". I went back to where my husband was waiting, and we just looked at each other. We couldn't even call our parents yet as we were so distressed. We couldn't even talk to each other; the words just couldn't come out. We held each other's hands waiting in anticipation for our son to return.

It felt like an eternity. We kept asking each other how long has it been now? What time is it now? It had been four hours now, and we thought he should be out of the theatre by now. The operation was five and a half hours. So many thoughts were running through my head. What if he doesn't survive the operation? What if there are complications? No, I can't think like that. Everything is going to be ok. The best surgeon in the country is carrying out the procedure. I dismissed those negative thoughts very quickly.

"Mum, Dad, are you ready to see your son? He is out now, and you will be glad to know that the operation was successful".

They warned us again to be prepared about the shock for so many wires were attached to him. I slowly opened the hospital doors, and there he was lying on the bed helpless. I burst into tears; they had to take me out. There was nothing I could do to help him. I felt that if I could take his place, I would do just that.

My daughter went back and forth to stay with my parents or my husband's family. She went to and from Manchester and Birmingham. During this difficult time, the school had allowed us to take our daughter out of school whilst the family looked after her. We both decided that it wasn't appropriate for her to see her brother straight away. She was only three years old, and she might get very upset. She was too young to comprehend what was going on. I called my mum and told her that in a few days they could all come up and see their grandson. I explained everything to my mum. I went back into room where my son was, and I couldn't stop looking at him. He turned his head and looked at me with a tear rolling down his face. This was heartbreaking, and there was nothing I could do. If I could have exchanged places with my son, I would have gladly done so; that thought kept going over in my mind. This episode in our life was a defining moment; it made a huge impact on us. All I could do was sit by his bedside and wait for him to recover.

My son's illness was one of the most painful experiences I had ever been through. I cannot even explain how distraught I was! This was one of the lowest and darkest points of my life. It was sixteen months of heartache and distress. I couldn't believe that the doctor had said that he was lucky to be alive! That they couldn't understand how he was still living! We realised he was our miracle baby! We would never forget this moment. My husband and I were so overjoyed that the operation was a success. No more trips to the hospital; no more waiting for him to choke. What a relief to know that our son was going to be fine.

This was not the end of it.

I will call this the 'valley experience'. What I was going through was made worse for me because I am not good at communicating my feelings. I internalise things because I always try to be strong. My whole countenance had changed, yet I could not hide the way I was feeling.

My workplace kindly gave me the time I needed off, so I could be with my son. They said to concentrate on your baby getting well, but I couldn't concentrate on anything else anyway!

It was difficult, but I had to try and look at the positives in this situation. Most of all I was grateful that our son was still with us, that he had made it through the operation. It could have been a different story; I could have been writing about a totally different experience.

Unfortunately, this was not the end of our trips to the hospital. The doctors said that he needed to have his throat stretched as it was smaller than the average and that he will have difficulties in swallowing. He was also born with a small hole in his nose, and tiny hairs would grow out of it. Frequently, my husband and I would have to squeeze his nose because his nose would get wider and puss and hair would come out. We accepted this as the norm and continued to do this for many years. One day my husband and I picked up our son from school, and we noticed that his face looked distorted. My son said a ball had hit his nose, so we decided to take him to the hospital. The nurse took the decision to drain his nose and investigated as to why puss was frequently coming out of his nose.

A few months later, we received a letter in the post for an appointment. Finally, we thought, they are going to sort his nose out. My son had a cyst growing under his nose which was growing each day. He was eight when they finally realised what was wrong. They had to perform a delicate procedure on his nose. They had to

OPEN DOORS

cut his nose open, so they could carefully remove the cyst. They then stitched his nose back up. He had to stay at home for two weeks; no school; no going out. He has been such a brave boy. He has been through a lot, and he is a fighter.

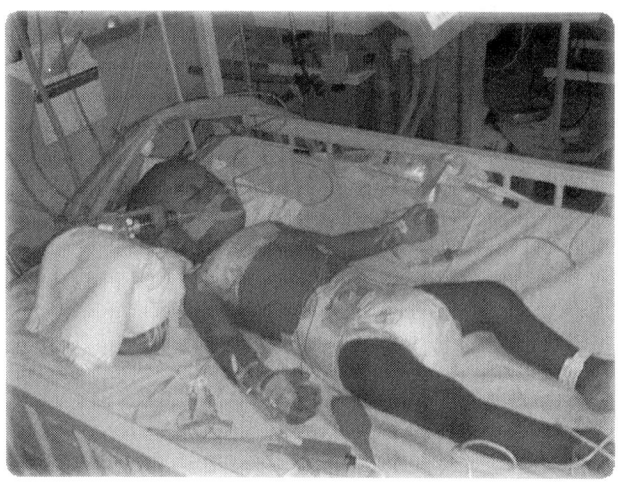

Chapter 9

Mission Completed

When I have my mind set on a particular thing, well in my case THINGS, I like a challenge. I just go for it. I remember thinking, I need to pass my driving test before my second baby arrives. I passed my theory, then I booked in for my driving test. Over the years I have stopped and started my driving lessons. But this time I was determined that I would finish what I had started. I was doing well. Sometimes my daughter would come with me on my driving lessons. She would sit quietly, well relatively quiet, in the back seat of the car with a book and her toys.

I had the date booked in for my driving test, and I felt I was ready for this. Well, my son decided to say hello to the world three weeks early. Instead of concentrating on the birth and the arrival of my baby boy, I was thinking about my driving test. There was NO WAY I was cancelling my test! I had come so far, I was going for it! I had not paid ALL that money for nothing. I started to weigh up the options. I made up my mind. Four days after giving birth I was ready to take the test. My mum was visiting for the week. "Right, Mum", I said, "I have breastfed the baby, I am ready to go now!"

OPEN DOORS

It was 7am; I got dressed and put on my black maternity dress as that was the only thing that fit me, plus it didn't need ironing. My driving instructor was eagerly waiting outside the car for me. "How are you feeling?" he asked. "Great", I replied, "I'm ready for this". He laughed and said, "I hope you don't have the baby on the wheel". I smiled and said, "No need to worry about that; I've had the baby as he came three weeks early! My mum is inside looking after him". He thought I was joking, but then he could see by my face that I was serious. He couldn't believe it, "Are you serious?" "You've had the baby?". "Yes, he's a beautiful baby boy weighing in at 5lb 1oz". "Let's get the show on the road!" I thought.

"Are you sure you are ready for this? We can postpone it; you have a very good reason to". "No, I'm ok."

I switched my phone on silent. My mum and husband had asked me to let them know how I had done when the test was finished.

Phew, the test was over. I was eagerly waiting to hear those words "You've passed". It seemed like forever for him to go over how he felt the test went and the minor errors I had made. Then I heard those three words that I really wanted to hear, "Congratulations you've passed". YES! I was over the moon. "Let me text my hubby and mum and let them know. No, let me keep them both in suspense". My instructor drove me home. He was overjoyed to know that I had passed as he knew how much it meant to me. We finally arrived home, and I gripped tight the certificate, thanked the instructor for everything and walked into the house. I couldn't get through the door quick enough. I had to compose myself, so I decided not to burst through the door. I put on a gloomy face, opened the living room door with a sad look on my face but I couldn't keep it up. "I've passed!" I said with excitement. The task was on to look for a car.

I was still at the school, but there came a point where I felt that it was time to move on. I'd been there for seven years. I thought that my mission, or my assignment, as I like to call it, was over. I thought looking for a new job would be easy. I'd been working as a teacher now for seven years. I had lots of experience so to me, finding a job would be no problem. Well, that's what I thought. I had to step back and think what job I wanted to do next or more to the point what job should I be doing next? So, I decided that I was going to work for a voluntary organisation. This was a massive step for me; a big change. People who know me, know that I DON'T like change. I like order, routines, systems and structures. However, I embraced this new beginning. New year, new start.

My new job title was Office Manager. As this was a new position, I had the privilege of writing my own job description. How fantastic is that? I felt at this point it was time for the organisation to go to another level. I set up systems and structures and put those in place, so the company could run more effectively. I didn't have all the solutions, but I knew what I wanted to see. The senior director always said, 'Do not come with problems; come with solutions.' What a great lesson to apply in your everyday life! So, I started to look for solutions.

The new job was great. I had my own office and was left to get on with the work that I had been set to do. I managed my own schedules. I loved it. It quickly dawned on me that this job is not about me and what I can do. It is about making links with the community. Letting the community know who we were and what we did. If we wanted to serve the community, we had to get our name out there. There is no better way to do this than by getting out there and meeting with different organisations in the area.

This job was not about having a new office or running my own schedules. It was about how I could best support the organisation in a meaningful way. It was about making a difference and making an impact in the lives of the service users.

I know what I'll do! I will make connections with the local College. I called the college and asked them if they could come in and run functional skills like Maths and English for the service users at the organisation. I told them the background of the organisation and the service users, and they were more than happy to come in and offer their services. This was great; the service users were excited about this new opportunity.

Let me tell you a little bit about the service users of the organisation I was volunteering for.

The service users had come from various backgrounds. A life of drugs, alcohol, criminal violence and much more. The college coming in and offering courses was a great way for the service users to start attaining skills for when they were ready to start employment. I started to reflect on my life and realised we came from two different worlds. I realised that we were the same too. Broken, hurting people and they needed some time out and for others to invest in them; give them direction and a sense of purpose. I had been broken and hurting because of rejection and people came and invested in me and helped me get up from where I was at. So why shouldn't I do the same?

The service users were mothers, fathers, business owners, homeowners and somewhere along the line they lost their way; lost their direction. The great thing about this organisation was that it was established to help broken people get their lives back together.

Things were going great at the centre. The men and women enjoyed the courses (most of the time). I had to constantly encourage some of the men and women and let them understand that these qualifications were beneficial to them. I explained why they needed it. It wasn't just about getting an education; it was teaching them that they have a purpose in life. I would often help the service users by putting a CV together for them, looking for jobs and encouraging to pursue their dream. I found great pleasure in helping people.

OPEN DOORS

I had to encourage them and let them know that the classes and qualifications were beneficial and would look great on their CV. Sometimes we have to do things, and we're not sure why we have to do it. Hopefully, later, the understanding will manifest. The college we had partnered with contacted me and asked if I would do some teaching in the community. I thought this was great as I believe you can never run away from your passion. I was born to teach. Not only to teach, but to make an impact. I always wanted to help the people I teach. It could be a friendly smile. I recall at a teaching conference, and the keynote speaker was encouraging the teachers that it is important to always greet your students with a smile because you may be the only friendly face that they see.

I always encourage my students at the start of new courses that anyone can start something, but the most important thing is to finish. This gives a sense of accomplishment and achievement. No one can take your certificates away from you. They are yours to keep. Your certificates are your passport to where you want to get to. Be proud of what you achieve. Things, or should I say barriers, will present themselves. Do not give up! Look for ways to overcome. When doing a course, unexpected things may occur. Do not quit though as you will only regret it. You must persevere because when you complete the course, you will be glad you did not give in. I always tell my students my story, we all have one. I choose to share it because I want my students to know that I didn't just stumble into a job. Or it was smooth sailing. I had challenges along my journey to get to where I am today. And just for the record I still have barriers that present themselves. I have learned to look and face things and know that you can overcome. It is not easy when you are in a challenging situation, but you can overcome if you want to. It is believing that you can. You must have the right support mechanisms around you to encourage you and point you in the right direction

QUITTERS NEVER WIN

I received a call from a friend about a great opportunity for our organisation to enter a competition and to possibly win £10,000. Wow! What a great opportunity to win £10,000 and use the money for a great cause. The 'Creme of Nature' competition was in its fourth year of the award. Creme of Nature was giving away £10,000 to community groups whose primary objective was to make a difference in the communities they served.

I contacted the organisation and asked how I could put our charity forward for the competition. I only had one day to fill in the application and send it off. No pressure! I filled out the questions then asked a friend to proofread the answers. In the excitement and rush, I'm sure that I had made some errors.

Eagerly checking my emails, I had a feeling that we would get through. A few days later, I opened my emails, and sure enough, we were through to the competition. Our organisation has been nominated to win £10,000. One of the questions that were asked was what would I do with the money if we won? I wrote that our organisation would spend the money on four particular areas:

1. Toilet facilities holiday disabled access
2. Renovate the community kitchen
3. Install a CCTV Security System to help combat vandalism
4. IT access and onsite training by buying a suite of computers. These improvements would be a catalyst in helping the service users to achieve their goals which would result in quality service for all.

I then had to write a short help blurb about what our organisation does.

'We help to build and restore the lives of individuals and their families who have been caught up in the vicious cycle of crime, gangs, drugs and alcohol addiction. To help us make a positive impact in our community simply text CAA to a particular number.'

Our organisation was one of the five finalists for the Creme of Nature action award 2011.

To vote for the community group, you wanted to win you had to have a UK mobile then you could vote and help make their dream come true. It was one phone number per one vote. You just had to text your vote, and it was completed, and if you had free texts, it was free.

I thought this was going to be an easy competition as all you had to do was to encourage people to text vote. To my astonishment, it wasn't easy! We worked so hard convincing people to vote for our organisation, and we had only four weeks to get the most votes. We had to pull together as an organisation. We got in contact with our sphere of influences and friends. But whatever we did, we just couldn't get from second place. I wasn't settling for second place! I did not enter the competition to come second. I thought I am in this competition as we have a great cause worth fighting for. Over the weeks we all tried hard, asking people to vote for the cause. It was exciting but challenging as we were struggling to get as many votes as the other organisation that was first place.

Time went by so quickly, and it was the last week of the competition. We still weren't in the top position. On the last day, we decided to hit the streets. I do not know why we did not think of that before. We designed flyers and took to the streets to hand them out. We thought this was a great opportunity to let the community, businesses and organisations know the great work that our organisation does. People were genuinely interested in the cause, and they were more than happy to vote for us. People were intrigued and wanted to know more about what we do and how they could support us.

It was time to pick the children up from school. They wanted me to stop off at the local shop so I could get them a treat. 'No can do! Mum is on a mission!' The children were used to me dashing around and helping out. I took them straight home with no delay. I dashed through the door, "Can't stop", I said to my husband. "This is the last day of the competition, and we are going out on the streets to get the votes". My husband laughed and looked at the children and said: "Mum is on a mission". I put my trainers on, got back in the car, met up with some friends, and we went for it! The strategy we thought would be effective was to stop people and let them know who we were and what we were doing for, and in, the community.

It was now 11:30pm, and it was very much past my bedtime. I was not going home without the mission being completed. We had been on the streets for more than six hours now. We had a passion and a cause, and we were putting our best efforts in. It was great to see the organisation members working as a team. This brought a great sense of community and unity. I distinctly remember one of my friends was out with us and carrying her laptop (it went everywhere with here). She was checking the votes, as you could check them online. We couldn't fathom why we were still losing even though the votes were going up significantly. It was approximately 1155 votes. We checked the votes again, and we realised we were now in the first spot. But the competition wasn't over until 12 midnight. We had five more minutes to get as many votes as we could. Someone shouted, "It is 12 o'clock! Let's check the votes!" To our amazement, we WON the competition! We did not win by a small majority; we won by a substantial amount. We were dumbfounded that we had actually WON! We were running up and down the streets shouting, "We did it! We did it!"

People were stopping their cars asking us what had happened. We were more than happy to share the good news. Yes, we did it! It was a team effort that we had all pulled together for, for this great cause. It is so important that you have the right people around you, so they can support you in what you are doing. It is all about helping others and looking beyond yourself. You as an individual can only do so much. But collectively we can do so much more. We proved that tonight, that TOGETHER, WE CAN!

The next day we were contacted by the organisation congratulating us on our win. He said, "I have one simple question. How did you manage to win? We were convinced that you would come second. Tell me the secret, honestly". I just simply said, "It was down to two things; teamwork and going out on the streets to let people know why they should vote for our cause".

My comment on receiving the award at the ceremony, went something like this,

"We were ecstatic and extremely grateful that we won the award as it took a lot of hard work! We joined together as a team going into our schools, universities, workplaces, and even on the streets getting the support of the local community, and in return, we are committed to making a massive positive impact on our community. In winning this award, we are now able to carry out

some of our great ideas that we have, to further drive improvements in our community."

We will use the Community Action Award for four important projects, provide on-site computer training, renovate the community kitchen, install a CCTV security system and improve toilet facilities to accommodate disabled access."

This was an unforgettable moment!

I stayed at the organisation for two and a half years, and in that time, I accomplished many things but most of all I learnt about myself and the power of making an impact in other people's lives. I still work for the organisation but on a voluntary basis. This charity is close to my heart, and I've been helping for eleven years to date.

Chapter 10

Making an Impact

Who would have ever thought that we would be saying our final goodbyes to my husband's mother, my mother-in-law, the children's grandmother? She was my mother-in-law for fourteen years. She was only 57 years old. So young. My mother-in-law left a remarkable legacy. Her life was an example to her family, her community and to her friends. Before my mother-in-law passed away, she received an award for her long-standing work in the community.

Let me share a few things that this incredible woman achieved in her life. She made a choice to make a difference and make an impact wherever she went and whatever she did. She was a foster carer for twenty-five years. She looked after so many children, providing them with a safe environment. She provided short-term and long-term care. The most important thing she provided was love. She treated the foster children just like her own children. Nothing was ever too much, she would always help, and if she couldn't, she would always find a way.

My mother-in-law had a larger than life character; very bubbly and out-going. Oftentimes we would go shopping, and she would randomly spark up conversations with complete strangers. Everywhere she went, everybody knew her.

She loved being around people, and people relished her company. I always remember her saying that she didn't have many friends. If her funeral was anything to go by, she was mistaken! They had to turn people away as the building became a fire hazard. There were over three hundred people packed in the building like a tin of sardines. People came from as far as America, and most of her foster children also came to say their final goodbyes. The day was so emotional and my mother-in-law's own mother was so distraught. She said that your children should not go before you. "I shouldn't be burying my daughter". There were no words of comfort in times like this. I just sat solemnly and listened. In times like this, we often want to say words that will comfort and soothe the individual. I have learnt to just say nothing, and just simply be there.

My mother-in-law was a superwoman. When we learned that she was ill in September of 2013, it shocked the whole family. It came as a huge shock! She became poorly very quickly; with countless trips to the hospital, seeing consultants, doctors and nurses. It was dreadful to see my mother-in-law in so much agony. She was helpless and needed personal care. She could no longer do many things for herself. It was our turn now to look after her. We found ourselves in an extremely difficult situation.

Seeing her in so much agony was heartbreaking. The doctors did all that they could do, but they made a decision that they were sending her home. We knew what that meant, but we thought maybe she could receive better care at home.

I remember one particular night after work, my husband and I picked up the children and went straight to Grandma's; that's what we called her. We went straight upstairs, and we would spend endless hours sitting by her bedside and attending to her needs. It was approximately eight in the evening, and we were ready to take the children home. I had this urge to stay a little bit longer. I said to my husband, "I think you should stay with your mum a little bit longer". "Why?" he asked. "I don't know, but I think you should". So, we stayed for another couple of hours. My husband did not leave his mother's side. He was reminding her of the times they had spent together and all the memories. I felt that this was the final goodbye.

We all said our goodbyes and went home and took the children to bed. The mood was low, which was understandable. We tried to stay in high spirits for the children's sake. We found this extremely difficult. Soon after we both went to bed, in the middle of the night, the phone suddenly rang. We knew what was coming next. My husband's brother-in-law was on the phone and said, "You need to come now". My husband quickly put the phone down and immediately went to his mum and dads house. By the time he arrived, she had sadly passed away. It was December of 2013. My husband called me to inform me of the news. I told him that when the children are awake, we will come straight over. We both decided that the children shouldn't go to school. We informed the school and told them what had happened. The school was saddened to hear the news as they had met her on several occasions when she came to pick up our children from school.

The pain of losing my mother-in-law was enormous. My children were eight and eleven years old at the time. Having to explain what had happened to Grandma to them, I couldn't bear thinking about.

Instead of asking why she had to go, we reminisce on the memories that she has left behind. We often talk about her, keeping her memories alive. That is what she would have wanted. She was a happy-go-lucky person and would brighten up people's lives. She always offered a helping hand. Not just to those whom she knew, but to strangers too. If she had it, she would give it. She lived her life for others and never thought just of herself.

She left behind a husband, three children and seven grandchildren. It made me think 'I MUST live a life that counts'. Live a life that inspires and encourages others. I want to make sure my life has purpose and meaning. With my mother-in-law passing away at such a young age, it made me pause and reflect. We do not know when our time is up, so it is important to live each day as if it is your last.

I sometimes wonder what people will remember about me when I'm gone? On this journey called life, we will meet many different people from all walks of life along the way. People come into our lives at different points, and I believe we should treat each person we meet with respect and kindness.

My mother-in-law was in my life for fourteen years. I learnt so many invaluable lessons from her, and she was an example to many. What will I make sure that I do to make an impact and a difference? Not just to my family but also to the people that I meet in various circumstances and situations? I wonder what impression I give to others? One thing I know for sure is that I want to be a positive influence on those I meet and interact with

MOVING ON

I had that urge again, to move on to my next assignment, but what would it be? I thought, "I know what I'll do. I'll go back into full time teaching" The search was on again to look for a job and I applied for many different jobs within the teaching sector but again, I couldn't find anything suitable or available. I decided to join an agency, and I'm glad I did! I received a phone call, and they asked me to email my CV. They called me the next day and said that they had found something that I may be interested in. I couldn't believe it! That was quick! They told me that that I would have to travel approximately 45 minutes to an hour to the destination and back. They told me the working hours and dates of the contract. The job sounded really great. It entailed teaching unemployed people and delivering courses so that they were equipped to carry out the role of a carer effectively.

The job interview was the following week, and I was told by the agency that there was only one position available and two people were shortlisted. My motto is, 'If it's meant to be, it will be'. I was next in line for the interview, and they asked questions. They informed me that the agency would be in touch. There was another lady who was also applying for the same position. We wished each other good luck.

I went home thinking 'I wonder who got the job', but it didn't matter because I just thought 'Whoever gets it, well, that's meant to be' and the other lady seemed really nice. I received a call from the agency later on that day, and they said they were pleased to say that I had got the job! They said we were both strong candidates and they didn't want to let either of us go! Wow! That was fantastic news! We would be working together! The job started the following week on a part-time basis which was perfect for me.

I was looking forward to starting work on the following Monday and meeting new people. The type of learners I would be teaching were the unemployed. I felt that this was a step for them to get the necessary qualifications needed and find employment. I went over to the main office in the morning and reported for duty. The lady that I had met was at reception waiting for me, and we both couldn't believe that they hired us both. We both introduced ourselves and knew instantly that we were going to get on very well. She had a story to tell; we all have a story; but it is whether we choose to share our past with others.

Over the next few months, we got to know each other very well. We would meet up in the half-term breaks. She met my children, and I met up with her daughter. She only had the one child. She started to open up to me about her past, and I was really intrigued by what she was saying. I thought, how does one person overcome all those obstacles? She was a very strong person, and she demonstrated that she had resilience. Resilience shows the strength of character, and she had the capacity to overcome. It showed me that she was an extremely strong character. Despite the adversity that was thrown at her, she had the strength to spring back. She chose to get up and fight back, and she was stronger for it.

I opened up and shared my life and my journey. We looked at each other and smiled and said we both have similar stories. We said to each other that wasn't it great that the agency had offered us both the job and there was only one position going. We both knew that we had met to help each other at this stage of our journey. Not just to help each other, but also to support the learners that we're going to be teaching. To give the learners that hope; that they can progress in life no matter what life has thrown at them.

This assignment was only to last for nine months as the provision was closing in the Summer, so I knew then that I had to start looking again for another job. At this new place, I met so many different people along the way they reminded me of the service users at the charity. Hurting, broken people wanting to better their lives but unsure as to how they would do it. I believe myself and my friends were there to support them on that part of their journey. It wasn't just about getting them a qualification. It was also about giving the students strategies and tips on what to do in a particular situation they found themselves in and where to get the help that they were entitled to receive. I felt so grateful at the end of the course. The students were so thankful and gave us cards, flowers and gifts of their appreciation. We were so overwhelmed with kindness that they showed us. They were so thankful for the support and guidance we gave them. I may never see those students again. However, I am pleased that I helped them along their journey.

Sometime later, a student that I was teaching from the previous job that I had left, shared with me how she was getting on after she had finished her course with me. Below is what she said:

'The number of certificates I've collected since I last saw you is unreal. I'm training to be a family support worker. I have my Level 3 in the certificate in Child Care now. That's my highest certificate up to now, and there are loads more that I have to do.'

I was overjoyed when she told me how much she has progressed since I last saw her. When she started on her journey with me, she enrolled on to a Level 1 programme. When she successfully completed the course, I encouraged her to progress onto the Level 2 with me. I knew she had the ability to achieve and she just needed that support and encouragement. Through her hard work and determination, she completed it, and she was elated. I always say, it is not how you start but how you finish. The key is to make sure that you complete whatever you have started. This gave her a sense of pride and achievement. Our paths may never cross again but knowing that she is on the right path and has made progress was enough for me.

When I hear stories of how people progress and move forward, it excites me! This particular learner faced many challenges and was unsure if she could make it through. It just goes to show that sheer determination and perseverance she could conquer anything. It allows you to focus on what you want and GO FOR IT!

The assignment was over, and the search for another job began again. The agency was on a mission to look for another job for me. This particular recruitment agency was fantastic! They were the ones who had found my last employment. They called me and guaranteed me that I would not be without a job for long. I attended a few teaching jobs; however, I was unsuccessful. By now I was just clutching at straws and applying for any teaching post. I had to pause and think, 'I do not want just any teaching posts'. I deeply thought about what area I wanted to teach in and the type of learners that I wanted to help. I wondered where I would end up. Weeks later I received a call from the agency. "I have found you a teaching job, and this position seems like it is just the job for you!"

I updated my CV and emailed it back to the agency. They sent my CV off and said they would contact me if they wanted me to attend an interview. The next day, I received a call, "They would like you to start work in four weeks' time, are you ok with that?" That wasn't a problem as I was not working. I was given brief information regarding the post. 'Ok', I thought, 'I will know the full details when I arrive I guess'.

Monday morning came around, and I was unsure what topics I would be teaching and at which level. All I knew was that I was teaching adults. I arrived in true 'ME' style. I had my Mary Poppins bag with all my teaching resources contained, ready to deliver anything! I met the manager in the foyer, and he had a beaming smile on his face. He was relieved that I had arrived. I later found out that I was the third teacher that the learners would have. As the previous teachers had left, they depended on me.

I was briefed about the learners, the topic and level I would be teaching. Also, the learners were to have two exams in the following January and had six weeks in which to revise. "Let me introduce you to the learners". We made polite conversation, and I was asked about my teaching background. We arrived at the classroom.

The learners were eagerly waiting for me to arrive. There were at least twenty-five learners packed into a computer room.

I was introduced to the class, and then the manager turned to me and said, "I will be in touch later to see how you are getting on".

Well! Talk about being thrown into the deep end! "Ok", I said with a raised voice. I was thinking on my feet. There weren't any teaching resources or books. I thought 'Let's just crack on with it'. Does this sound familiar to any teacher?

I introduced myself and talked about my background and my previous employment. Then I asked the class to do the same. This was going to take a while as there were so many learners in the class. Then, for the rest of the lesson, we played 'catch up'. The learners depended on me to get them through the course. My mission was to get the learners through the course. This was a big task, but I made sure that I followed through and helped them complete the course. I wanted to show them that they could achieve anything, despite the difficulties. When they completed the course, they were so proud of their accomplishments. I knew they could do it!

I embraced the opportunities that came my way at work. I was privileged to write a full degree programme alongside my two colleagues. Once approved, it was accredited by Sheffield Hallam University. It was challenging as we were tasked to write it alongside teaching full time. However, we managed to complete it. What a great opportunity!

As I got to know the learners, they shared with me many heart-breaking stories about their lives. I was surprised that they were so open. I concluded that they just wanted to be heard. These were stories of heartbreak, obstacles, tough times and struggles. But there was a theme running throughout them all. 'OVERCOMING'. Despite their valley experiences, they did not let their situations define them or live with a defeatist attitude. I would encourage them with words of comfort. 'Yes, it is ok to cry and scream but channel it in a positive way. It is so important to manage your emotions, do not suppress or ignore them. Deal with them, you may find that it will benefit you to go and seek professional help, confide in a friend. Most importantly TALK about how you are feeling.'

Positive self- talk is also another key to unlocking any pain you are going through. Do not embrace negative talk such as 'I can't get through this, I will never get over it'. Through your challenges, you WILL be stronger! Speak positive words to yourself and take one day at a time.

Do not let your circumstances define who you are. Have that belief in knowing that you can do anything if you put your mind to.

Learn from your pain. I believe we go through things for a reason. In life things will happen that are beyond our control or the unexpected will happen. But you must learn from your pain. I recall we received some devastating news regarding my husband's uncle. An unfortunate incident occurred, where he was viciously attacked and left for dead. We went to the hospital to see how he was. Nothing could prepare us for what we saw! I wanted to break down and cry. My husband turned and looked at me and whispered, "He looks so much like mum". I had to be strong for my husband. His uncle was his mum's brother. I had to hold in my own pain and shock as the pain on my husband's face was excruciating to see. I knew what he was thinking. I replied, "He WILL get through this". His uncle was unconscious and tied to many tubes. The doctor's report was negative. They were giving us their medical opinion. Even though the report was gloomy, the family chose to remain hopeful and stay positive. When we went to visit him, we would talk about the good times.

I distinctively remember at Christmas; my husband's uncle came to visit. The festive season was in the air; fun and laughter filled the room. His uncle had a great big smile on his face and a bag in his hand filled with presents. How sweet, I thought, that he had bought his niece and nephews Christmas gifts. He gathered all the children around and placed the gifts on the table, accompanied by Sellotape and wrapping paper. I was watching, as I was very intrigued with what he was doing. He asked the children what present they would like. Very excitedly, they chose their gifts. He then proceeded to hand them wrapping paper and Sellotape. He told them they can wrap their own gift! The children thought this was great and they were eager to wrap their presents. The whole room burst into laughter. Only he could get away with that! What a great guy! My children still talk about it today, and it is still as funny as it was then.

Nearly a year has passed, and my husband's uncle has made massive progress. He is now conscious. He can sit up and recognise the family. He is not the same man as he used to be, but he has come a long way. He chose to fight; each day was an upward struggle. But through his sheer determination, he is on the road to recovery. There is still a long way to go, but you have to keep taking a day at a time. You cannot rush any process, you have to go through it. Having supportive family around him, I believe, has aided and enabled him to get through his adversity.

LIFE BEGINS AT 40

How did I get to this age? Reaching forty was a turning point in my life. Time has flown by so quickly! When I was 39 years old, I was mentally preparing myself to reach the 'BIG 4-0'. This was a big thing for me. Saying goodbye to my Thirties and embracing my Forties. It made me reflect on my life and what I have achieved. I call this counting my blessings. I have an amazing husband, and we are approaching our eighteen-year anniversary. We have two fantastic children. The eldest will be going to college in September, and my youngest will be starting High School in September. These are huge transitions and an exciting new part of their journey. We are still in the house that initially caused us so much grief, but now it is our home. We have been living here for over fourteen years. We are now contemplating if we should sell the house and move. Decisions, decisions, decisions!

My cousin called me and asked if I would like to go on a mini cruise with her. She is six weeks older than me, so we wanted to celebrate our 40th birthday together. 'Let's do it', so we went ahead and planned it. We had an amazing time, and we laughed so much, it reminded us of when we were children. We were carefree. Our children were staying with family, and our husbands were left at home. We were free to enjoy each other's company and just relax and have fun. We will definitely be doing that again!

I celebrated my birthday all year, just because I could! Getting older and wiser (I hope), being forty was not so bad. My daughter thinks I'm old. She said she is NEVER telling her friends how old I am. I just laughed because I remember when I was her age and I said the same thing to my mum.

I was happy to have reached this stage of my life. I have faced many challenges in my life and some I have chosen not to mention. I have worked through hurt, pain and disappointment, knowing that I WILL overcome. My mum, who is my rock, taught me how to deal with the storms in my life. My husband always believed in me, even when I didn't believe in myself. My step-dad always encouraged me to chase my dreams and not to settle for the mediocre.

BEAUTIFUL FLOWER

Losing two significant people in my life caused me so much pain.

'Flower' was the meaning of my auntie's name.

Firstly, losing my auntie, my mum's only sister, was so horrendous; the pain was so intense. She was only 60 years young. I received a phone call from my mum which was nothing out of the ordinary. What was to come next was devastating. "Your auntie is in hospital." My mum went on to explain what was happening and what was wrong with my auntie. I didn't hear any more of the conversation. I thought 'This can't be happening!' All sorts of thoughts were running through my mind. I just couldn't believe what I was hearing. I was close to my auntie, and we had a great relationship. We used to reminisce about times when I was a child and the things that she used to say to me as I was growing up.

I won't go through the details of the coming months, but I'm sure that you can get the picture. It was a harrowing time. Endless trips to the hospital; visitors coming around the house. I visited as often as I could as I was living in a different city and working full time.

On the weekend that I was going down to visit my auntie, I received another phone call. It wasn't good news. I couldn't hold it in, and tears were streaming down my face. I didn't have the words to speak. My children have never seen me this way. I would go to my room, sit on the edge of the bed and just sob. On receiving the news of her illness to her passing away was a matter of months. I cannot explain how I felt. I was in a daze. People were talking to me, but I couldn't hear. I somehow managed to block the noise out, and I was in my own little world.

My auntie was an amazing woman. She was a 'legend'. If you had met her, you would know exactly what I mean. In some ways, she reminded me of my mother-in-law. Kind-hearted, generous and loving, just to name a few of her qualities. They are both no longer here to see my children grow up. I always make sure that their memories live on. We have countless conversations about them and reminisce and look at the photos. We even look back at video camera footage.

I learnt a lot from my auntie. She raised four amazing children. They are grown up with families of their own. She had a very good work ethic; she was extremely hard working and generous. She faced many challenges but did not let that stop her achieving what she wanted in life. She had the attitude of getting up from where she was at and moving forward. It wasn't always easy, but she was determined. Determination will get you to that place that you never thought you could reach. It was at her funeral where I heard of all the challenges she had gone through; the pain and the heartache. It was humbling to hear, that despite what came her way she did not let that deter her from where she was going. On hearing the impressive eulogy, I thought you can either go through life having a victim mentality, allowing situations to overtake and consume you. Or, you can change your perspective. Life is all about perspective. It's how you look at things (circumstances or situations). You MUST focus on the positive and your life will feel much more enriched. It is imperative to change your outlook.

My auntie did just that. She made a positive choice; she made a firm decision that she was moving forward. What a great lesson to learn from a great legend!

Another legend in my life was a great man that I had known for ten years. He passed away suddenly and was only in his thirties. I am not going to go into the details of what happened, but what I learned about his life is important.

Let me take you back to when we met this great legend. Let me tell you how my husband and I met him.

My husband and I joined a voluntary organisation back in the year 2007. It was like one great big family. That is where we met this great legend. When our son was critically ill, he heard the news and came down to the hospital. We had only known him for a few weeks. He was very supportive during the time of our loneliness.

What a nice guy I had thought. He was always asking how our son was doing. Also, if we needed anything we just had to ask. From that day, we knew that this guy had a big heart and we remained friends with him and his wife. They were made for each other, and they always had time out for us. Over the years a friendship grew and grew.

This legend always looked out for me and my family. He had a soft spot for my son as he was there at the time of his sickness.

He would sometimes look after my children and take us out for meals. He not only showed kindness to me and my family but also to friends and even strangers.

Money was no object to him. He lived by a basic principle, 'Do unto others that you would have them do to you'. Not only to me did he give financially but also, he gave up his time. He was a big kid at heart; a lovable character, nothing was a problem. He always wanted to help wherever he could. I heard so many amazing things that he did with his life and what he did for others.

At the funeral, a few people spoke about the impact he had on their lives. We were so moved to hear these stories. His life impacted so many people! Even today, I still hear stories of what he has done for people. There are so many things that I have learnt from him. Two things stand out. Firstly, he was very generous, and secondly, he had no hidden agenda. He would always go out of his way to make sure that he helped those that were in need. He left an amazing legacy, and I miss him dearly. The day before he passed away, I remember seeing him, and he said to me, with a cheeky grin on his face, "Smile". He always said that to me. It always made a chuckle.

He was successful in everything he did. Yes, he had failures along the way. He picked himself up and started again. He learned valuable lessons from his mistakes. He had his own business and employed recovering addicts. He helped single parents, and he would put on amazing activities for children. He was an outstanding cook! He could cook any cuisine. He always had people around at his house, and he was a 'feeder'. He made sure that you would take food home with you too!

He had a change of direction; his journey has not always been a smooth one. He started with a little, but he chose to get the right path and make a difference in his life. He made an impact that would change people's lives forever.

The many people that were impacted by this great legend are now asking themselves, what does my life say about me? I think it is important to live a life that has purpose and meaning.

What legacy are you going to leave behind? It is not about the money you have or the house and the cars. These material things will fade away.

It's about how you lived your life and the difference you made in people's life. That's what will last; that is what people remember.

In honour of his legacy, I was asked to be a trustee of the foundation that has been set up in his honour to continue his legacy. "Of course!" I quickly replied. What a privilege to be asked, and, to be a part of this great venture! I believe in 'paying it forward'.

Chapter 11

Long Lost Families

"I met this young man at your Grandmother's funeral", my mum said, as we were driving to the local shop. She was referring to my biological dad's mum who had passed away. There was clearly more to this story than she was letting on.

As my mum proceeded with the conversation, I wondered where this was going. My mum continued to speak about my grandmother's funeral. As this young man had continued to speak, she was curious as to who he was as she had never met him before. The way he was speaking, she had thought he must be a grandchild, but who was the parent?

She asked someone "Who is that person who is speaking?"

"Let me introduce you to him."

To my mum's surprise, it was my biological dad's son! In fact, there were three sons present at the funeral! As my mum was speaking to the young man who made the speech at the funeral, she could see the similarities between myself and him.

My mum thought to herself, I am finally meeting and actually talking with one of my daughter's siblings!

So, my mum properly introduced herself to him. She told him all about me. The conversation flowed naturally. She felt as if she had known him all her life. My mum and dad spoke to him like he was one of their own children.

Driving home from the funeral, my mum thought that I would have to know about the brothers! She wasn't scared to tell me. However, she did not want to upset me. My mum asked her husband to speak to me about it. Things happened so quickly that he never got the chance to do so. My brother was so curious about me and had said, "Do you think she will meet me?"

My mum didn't answer the question directly, but she replied, "Let me speak to her". They exchanged telephone numbers, and my mum said she would be in touch.

My mum continued to tell me that he was just like me. He had my temperament, personality and my wit. I thought, 'Goodness, another me in the world!' I just couldn't even imagine it.

I grew up as an only child, and I loved it. My mum reminded me that I once said to her that she should not have any more children because I didn't want to share my things. To discover at the age of 40 that I had three brothers and that I am the oldest of them all was a surprise!

Why now? Why at this stage of my life? I had closed the door to my dad's past and now had moved on. Well, so I thought. I soon realised that the door was not shut to my past. The door was open, but I chose not to walk through it. I had planned that I would continue my life without knowing my dad. Reflecting on this, that was how I chose to deal with it. But I learned I hadn't dealt with it properly. I chose to ignore it. But as the years went on, I managed my emotions and went through a healing process. Personally, if I had not dealt with my past, I would not have wanted to meet the other members of my family.

As the children were growing older, they would always ask questions about the family they didn't know. My daughter would ask most of the questions as she is extremely inquisitive.

I didn't have any answers to give them. All they knew was that my mother and my nan raised me. My dad did not want to know me, and I left it there. My daughter just could not understand why. All I could say to her was that people make choices and he has made that decision. You have to move on.

Through the years I learnt how to deal with my emotions. As I got older, I decided to forgive my dad. I may never see him, but I knew in my heart that I did not want any bitterness or resentment toward him.

The past is the past. We make choices and decisions which affect our future. I did not want those negative feelings to affect me or my children. I didn't just arrive at this decision. It took years to deal with it. Growing up without my biological father made me have lots of questions. I knew I would never know the answers, so I decided not to dwell on it too much.

Coming to the realisation at forty years of age, that I no longer held negative feelings for my biological dad, is when I met my brothers. It wasn't until I had let go of the past, my feelings and my negative outlook towards my dad that I could open the door to embrace my brothers.

My mum said, "Do you want to meet him?" "Yeah, ok". I think she was shocked by the response. I knew if I never met him I would go home and ponder if I had made the right choice. For me, this was a brave step. I am the type of person that would often have to go away and process things before making a decision.

We were in the clothes shop, and my mum called him. I had all sorts of emotions, and so many questions were running through my mind. Should I go back home? My mum said, "He lives around the corner from where we are, and he is on his way!"

Oh dear! That was when I went into panic mode! I called my husband and told him. He was excited, and so were the children.

We waited and waited. He called my mum to let her know that he was stuck in the football traffic. I kept on looking at different people wondering is that him.

Someone else would walk past. I thought, that may be him. I had no idea of what he would look like. Will he be short like me? Will he have big eyes like me? Will he have chubby cheeks? Finally, he arrived. A guy was walking towards us with a big smile on his face. That's him! He was nothing like I had imagined. He was tall, yes, but with big eyes and chubby cheeks.

We took one look at each other and gave each other a massive hug. It was so emotional; I couldn't believe I was hugging my brother! We couldn't stop staring at each other. We look so much alike.

It usually takes a while for me to get used to strangers; however, it felt so natural talking with him. We had questions to ask each other, and we soon realised that we had the same upbringing. I couldn't describe the feeling, after forty years finding out that I had brothers. And here I am, face to face with one of my brothers. I'm the oldest, and this episode in my life felt like the programme 'Long Lost Families'. Imagine finding out that you have siblings later in life! My mum sat with us and smiled. She was so happy that I had embraced my brother!

I know that if I had met him years before it would have played out differently. This is because I was still on my journey; from rejection, hurt and brokenness to complete healing. I had to deal with all the negativity before embracing the future. I wasn't sure how I would feel when I met him, but I was glad when I did. I needed to open the door of opportunity. We soon learned that we have a lot in common. I knew my children and my husband would welcome him into the family. It was strange as now my children had an uncle. We both made a decision to work on our relationship, so we could get to know each other. We agreed it would be great to meet up again and conversed together, "We have so much to catch up on! It'll take all of our lives!"

I thought why not! Why, after all this time, had our paths crossed? Who knows? But we both made a decision that we would leave the past behind and move forward. We thought, 'Let us embrace the future and be glad that we have found each other!' The one thing I quickly realised was that he was the chatterbox. He couldn't stop talking! I thought maybe it was nerves. I've since learned it wasn't nerves; he talks A LOT! Now, I'm not a good conversationalist, especially when I meet someone for the first time. I am a processor, and I was spending time working him out. We exchanged numbers and said that we would meet up again over the Summer.

We met up again, and I was also able to get to know my other two brothers and their families. I had nieces and nephews! I couldn't believe it! We chatted and laughed together. There were two things we all had in common; the eyes and the sense of humour.

During the summer, the brother that I met for the first time came to visit me. It didn't seem real that I was actually going to meet him at the train station. We spent the day together catching up laughing, and I showed him lots of photographs. We got to know each other quite quickly as we spent all that Summer on the telephone together. We had so much to say and so much to share. Even to this day we still have a lot of chats and laughs and meet up when we can. This was a door I chose to walk through. A door to my past. I knew the door wasn't closed it was just that I had decided to carry on with my life. There came the point in my life where I faced the negative and viewed things differently. That was when I knew that things were going to change because I decided to change. Things happen for a reason, but as you are going through it, you don't view it that way. I am looking forward to getting to know my siblings.

I remember when I met my brother for the first time. It was the Summer of 2016 to be exact. I had not too long turned 40 years old. I felt that something super exciting was going happen that year as I reached the grand age of 40. I never in my wildest dreams thought that I would discover I had a brother! I was an only child for my mum. I wasn't raised by my dad.

When I was asked if I wanted to meet my brother, I responded with a YES very quickly. I didn't want to think about it as I may have changed my mind (I was good at that). But, I wasn't going to allow my past to define my response.

When we met, we both bonded immediately. Obviously, we had so much to share with each other. I'm glad I responded in a positive way because we get on so well and now have a beautiful relationship. If I had closed the door to my past, I wouldn't have had the opportunity to meet my little brother. He is 3 years younger than me, and he loves to call me the 'ELDER' sister. We now have the rest of our lives to get to get to know each other, and that is such a beautiful thing. The power of your response can change your direction.

My brother's account of meeting me, his sister, for the first time.

I was standing with my brother at the wake of my Grandmother (that I never knew) and my Auntie and suddenly a lady that I was unfamiliar with approached us and asked, "Who was a lecturer?" So, I looked at my brother and thought, "How does she know that." I then replied, "me" and the lady said," I'm your Mum". At the same time, we both said, "Who?" and she replied ever so calmly, "I am your sister's mum!" (with a smile on her face). Well, I don't know about my brother (I turned and looked at him, and he turned and looked at me same time), but by now my whole body went hollow, and all I could think was "Say what!?" I was very happy and at the same time asking myself, "Is this for real?" I had previously learned that I had an elder sibling maybe around five to six years before this day. Anyway, we sat down, and the lady was introduced to my sisters Pops (nice chap), and we all had a chat. We had some delightful conversations, to say the least, and very informative. I also learned that I had a niece and nephew that are doing very well too (joy to my heart). Also, I learned about my sister and her husband's wedding. Just beautiful!

OPEN DOORS

I asked what my sister was like and her step-dad replied, "If you want to know what your sister is like, just look in the mirror. You talk alike, both direct to the point and look alike". I just smiled thinking (you mean she looks like me).

After the funeral, I was very eager to meet my sister, to say the least. And truthfully, as each day went by I thought maybe we may not ever meet, but I could understand why it may be that way. There is one thing I know for sure though, and that is, The Almighty is more than good! So, I held on to that very thought. My sister's mum would keep in contact with me via texts letting me know how my sister, brother-in-law, niece and nephew were doing. The more I heard from my sister's mum, I just knew that my dream would come true! And it did!

Saturday 30th July 2016; I can remember it like it was yesterday. My beloved Aston Villa team was playing Middlesbrough, and I had just got ready to go out to meet my friends. A short time later, my phone rang, and when I looked at the screen, it was my sister's mum. Instantly, I started smiling. For some reason, this day did not feel like my normal day. But I just could not understand the feeling. I answered, and my sister's mum asked if I was busy? For some strange reason I said no, but in fact, I did have things to do. On the inside, I started to feel nervy, but in a pleasant way (don't ask me why!). She then said: "I am at One Stop shop in Perry Barr with your sister; would you like to meet up if you're not busy?" Well, I froze and paused. One thought was spinning around my head "Did I just hear right?" Let's just say I replied "Yes! For sure. On my way!" I called a taxi straight away. The football traffic was really bad and took me well over an hour to get there.

In the taxi, all I could think was "Wow! I am meeting my elder sister." This felt strange but in such a nice way. The traffic was terrible, and I remember thinking "What if they have to leave, please God keep them there. Please!" Because of my various health issues, I was thinking, "Why could it not have been when I was in good health when we meet?" My health means a lot to me, and I didn't want my sister picking up that I was not well (as it is something I don't really talk about). It is what it is I guess. These feelings I'm having though! Yes! For the first time, I was a little nervous. Maybe a little anxious too. But it sure felt good. "Wow! I'm going to meet my sister. OH YEAH!"

I got out of the taxi and was walking in the direction to meet them. When I looked up I saw two ladies standing there; one had her back to me. Straight away I thought is that my sister facing me, is it? No? Yes! The closer I got, the more I just knew it was. To recognise yourself in someone else is very frightening, in a nice way though. I walked up, hugged and kissed her and thought 'Yo! This is my sister, very small though'. Hahaha! Then I said "Hi". We went for some food, and it was just amazing to see how much we are alike and had in common; our physical features and so on. Even though it was very real, it was also very overwhelming. Don't ask me why; maybe nerves for real! All good though. We took some pictures and all that jazz and had some over-standing *conversations. After forty-five minutes we exchanged numbers and went our separate ways.*

Walking away with the biggest smile on my heart was just what the doctor ordered. I went away with the biggest smile ever, and it stayed with me. Everyone who went past me was looking as if to say, "What are you so happy about?" I just continued to smile because one of my dreams had more than come true! 'Give thanks' is all I could think of!

I recall phoning my brothers to let them know I had just met our sister. Questions and conversations were flowing in full effect for days. All very good indeed.

My sister and I would call each other every day. Literally speaking from morning until night and right through it. Hahaha!

It was all good though, as we were getting to know one another just swell! There was more than a lot in common (sayings and phrases). The one phrase my sister can keep for sure is "stop the bus!" But I love it. After spending what now feels like the whole of the school summer holiday on the phone and more, were all then blessed with the opportunity to spend a day with each other at my beautiful sister, brother-in-law, niece and nephews house. THERE REALLY IS NOTHING LIKE FAMILY LOVE AND APPRECIATION. A true blessing indeed.

All these new family experiences have given me more determination and inspiration to fight off my symptoms.

EACH DAY REALLY MEANS THAT LITTLE BIT MORE. It sure does!

The way I feel now is as simple as this. "Now I have met my sister and family, I never wish to be without them. It has been one of the biggest inspirations I have ever had."

FAMILY LOVE "A TRUE BEAUTIFUL FEELING AND NOTHING BUT LOVE AND RESPECT FOR THEM ALL"

Me and my little brother

OPEN DOORS

On our life journey, there are many doors of opportunity. However, sometimes things do not work out. Does that mean the door is closed and you should not pursue the opportunity? Or is it not your time yet to walk through that door? I decided to walk through many doors that were open to me. Before taking the different opportunities, I reflected and thought about whether I should walk through the door.

So, my journey continues. I wonder where this journey will take me. I wonder what lies ahead? Who knows? What I do know is that life a beautiful journey. I will learn from the past and see the positive. It is all about perspective. I will embrace the future with anticipation knowing that great things await me. I will look at every 'door' in my life in a positive way.

Consider your own journey and the decisions you have made and will make. The door is open; the possibilities are endless!

Chapter 12

Keys to Leading a Motivated Life

Living a motivated life is one of the keys to living a positive, focused life. Doors of opportunity will open when you least expect it. Staying motivated and positive can sometimes be difficult when situations are looking bleak. I want to share my keys on how I live a motived life.

It is important to decide to be more proactive and make positive choices as this will change the course of your life.

I learned that gliding through life and doing the usual activities would not benefit me in terms of making my dreams become a reality.

Does this sound familiar?
Get up and get ready for work.
Getting the children up for school.
Preparing the sandwiches for all the family.
Dropping the children off at school.
Travelling to work.
Teaching... (depending on your line of work)
Going home...
I think you get the picture.

You have to work hard on your goals. You have to pursue them. You may be working on your goals and dreams but suddenly find that because of everyday life you are only making very tiny steps. By the end of the year, surprise, surprise, you realise that you have not made much progress.

Make a decision to **GET UP** and **GO** after your dreams. You will be glad that you decide to make that choice.

Since I made that decision, I have made so much progress towards my goals! There are so many doors of opportunity that have presented themselves! I am so surprised that things are moving at such a rapid pace!

When I decided to take that initial first step, I noticed so many people wanting to support me with my goals. Wow, I felt so blessed. It was, and continues to be, a very exciting time! Decide that this is the year when you will see your dream come true! Remember, you have to make steps towards your goals and dreams. It will NOT just happen.

I will share with you how I made progress this past year.

It all started with me making a decision that I was going to pursue my goals.

I had always been told that I should write a book. I thought about it, but then, that thought disappeared very quickly. Then on the 1st Jan 2018, I decided that I would go for it. I have not stopped writing since the start of the year!

Guess what? On the 9th February of 2018, I finished writing my book whilst also working full time in a very demanding job. I'm a lecturer and a mother of two. My daughter is fifteen and leaving school this year. My son is eleven and will be attending High School in September. I also work for a voluntary organisation during the week. I have been stretched to capacity, but I was on a mission; a mission to make it happen. No one was going to do it for me.

ACT– Take Action and do something!

Come with me on a motivational journey.

I have many dreams in life, and I'm sure you have too. But in order for my dreams to become a reality, I live by 3 steps.

KEY 1
See it.
Plan it.
Anticipate it.

To see something, you have to visualise it. You have to see what it is that you want to do. You have to see the end result, then work backwards. By taking this approach, it will give you a clear focus.

Then you have to plan it. In order to know where you are going, you have to plan it out. Let me use travelling as an analogy. You have seen where you want to travel to. Then you plan what you are going to do each day. Or, you have some idea of what you want to do. Once you have made your plans, you then put the steps in place.

You then look forward to travelling; you anticipate it. You can imagine what the holiday is going to be like. You can see the activities that you will be doing, or the places you are going to visit. This brings excitement, and you cannot wait to get there

So, what is your dream? I challenge you to go out and buy a journal and write down your goals and dreams. Taking this action will give you clarity on the journey ahead. See it, plan for it, then anticipate it.

As we journey through life, we travel with different equipment. WHAT! Yes, we travel with different equipment. We sometimes carry around resentment, rage or regrets. This can allow the journey to become longer and may take you off course. BUT, we don't always carry around negativity. It can also be positive things, which produces positives vibes. I call this the 'feel good' factor.

KEY 2
Dare to Dream BIG #DTDB

Here are a few tips to see your dreams come true.

- Share your dreams with your peers. It is great to talk to others, so they can support you along the way, and vice versa.
- Write your dreams down, this is very important. Make it very explicit. This ensures that you have a clear direction, and it will inspire you to move forward.
- Have small milestones. This will make your dreams more manageable and achievable.
- Do NOT give up, even when you feel your dream is unachievable, or it is taking too long.

In order to progress in life, we need to carry the necessary items in order to live a much happier life, and this got me thinking.

Reflection

What equipment do we need to get rid of so that our journey is lighter?

What do you need to focus on to stay on track?

There are so many things you can focus on, but here I will mention '**DREAMS and GOALS**'

OPEN DOORS

What steps are you taking to make your dreams and goals a reality?
Here, let me share a few tips.
Each day I do something towards my dream.
- I share what I have done with a small group of friends.
- I have a tick list.
- I spend a certain amount of time on my daily tasks.
- Each day I set myself small goals and follow through with these goals.

The key is doing things in bite-size chunks. This is important as it makes it more manageable. These goals must be 'SMART.'

S-pecific
M-easurable
A-chievable
R-ealistic
T-imely

Are your goals SMART? If not, pause and think about what changes you need to make, so your dream become more realistic.

KEY 3
BEWARE OF HINDRANCES.

Have you come across any hindrances to achieving your dreams yet?

I have. The biggest one so far. **DISTRACTION.**

There are so many distractions around. Facebook, Instagram, Twitter. They all have their uses; however, they can be our biggest distraction. It could be something else for you, but we all have some distractions. The question is, how do we tackle the distractions; how can we be more productive? We all have 24 hours in our day, but it is how we manage our time which is important.

- Set yourself a particular time when you will be working on your dream. Stick to it as this will become your 'dedication timeslot'.
- Have a particular place where you will work on your dreams and goals.
- Switch off your phone! Just checking that one text can become a whole conversation. Then before you know it, it is time to pick up the children, pick up the suit from the dry cleaners, etc., etc.!
- Take one day at a time. You may want to buy a diary, so you can write down your goals, and then you tick them off once you have achieved it. This will give you a sense of achievement.

- Do not make excuses for not doing what you have set out to do.

KEY 4
STAY FOCUSED AND STAY IN THE ZONE.

What are you going to do to stay focused?

Do not let people distract you from your focus. You know what you need to accomplish to get ahead. There will come periods of times where you feel discouraged and disappointed. This is part of the journey. You will have your high moments where you are feeling on top of the world and that you can conquer anything that comes in your way. I call that the mountaintop experience, the 'I can' attitude. Nothing is going to stop you!

Then you will get the down times where you feel you are not making any progress. You may feel like quitting as the plans you are making don't seem to be making progress. You cannot seem to make it. I call this the valley experience. You just want to be on your own and isolate yourself from friends and family. This is when you HAVE to push even harder to continue to move forward. Pursuing your goals will not come easy, you have to be persistent. If you really want to do something you WILL have to work in order to achieve.

So, are you willing to work hard and pursue your goals? You have two options:

1. **QUIT** - this option is very easy.

It is easy to give up and walk away from pursuing your goals. No one achieved anything by doing that. You will not get ahead with a defeatist attitude. Don't be that person that never finishes anything. A client once said to me, "I am good at quitting and never finishing anything". Well, if that is you, change your attitude and say, 'I believe, I can' as this will change your outlook. You can't just say it once. This is a daily confession, believing that from now on, whatever you set out to do, you will accomplish it!

2. **PURSUE** - now that is the difficult option, especially when you feel like your plans are not going according to plan.

Take one step at a time; keep thinking about why you are doing what you are doing. Ask yourself

"How will this make me feel once I have achieved what I have set out to achieve?"

For every milestone, you complete, reward yourself, as this gives you a sense of accomplishment.

KEY 5
PERSPECTIVE.

I believe in life, it is how you look at things. You must focus on the positives because that way your life will feel more enriched. It is important that you change your outlook. Do not look at what you haven't accomplished. Look at what you have achieved so far. Start to think in a different way.

Start afresh! Don't wait for the New Year. Start NOW! What you should be focusing on is, "What do I want to accomplish this year?"

I dismissed the class, "See you guys tomorrow" with a great big smile on my face. It was the end of the day, and I was feeling exhausted.

About fifteen minutes later a student walked back into the class. I thought she may have forgotten something. She walked up to me and said, "I got you this."

It was a small black diary. On the front, it read '**My Goals**'. I eagerly opened it (I love things like that), and it read '**A goal without a plan is just a wish**'. "LOVE IT", I said with a beaming smile on my face. Wow! That is a powerful statement.

I quickly thanked the student for this lovely gift. She had also bought herself one.

This told me that she must be thinking about her goals too. What a great way to start the year! Start as you mean to go on.

Further inside the book, you had to write down the following:

- **Your goals.**
- **Why is the goal important?**
- **Steps in order to achieve your goal.**
- **When you must achieve this goal.**
- **What will the reward be once you have achieved it?**

On the proceeding pages, it had a goal tracker. You then had to write down your weekly steps and tick if you have achieved it or not. Then it left a space for you to write your notes.

What are your goals for this year?

Change your perspective.

As the proverbial phrase says: 'Is the glass full, or half empty?'

KEY 6
MAKING AN IMPACT

"Oh, my word! How lovely to hear from you!"

"Happy New Year and how are you?"

"I most certainly do remember you! I've still got that book you gave to me, and I have read it; it was excellent."

"The number of certificates I've collected since I last saw you is unreal. I'm training to be a family support worker, and I have my Level 3 in childcare now. That's my highest certificate up to now, there are loads more that I have gained too."

"Thank you so much for getting in touch. I have been thinking about you and wondering if you're still at that College?"

"You take care and email me whenever you want."

What a lovely email I received from a past student. You never know the lives that you affect!

KEY 7
OVERCOMING

Do not let your circumstances be a barrier to prevent you from overcoming the challenges you may find yourself in.

I was teaching the students about barriers that you may face. They came up with some fantastic examples:

- Past
- Life
- Circumstances
- Environment

Barriers can prevent you from unleashing your potential. It can become a stumbling block and distort your vision. It can then become a distraction. You can either do one of two things.

You can allow the barriers to block your future, and then you become stagnant. You will then become ineffective and feel that your life has no purpose.

Or you can overcome the barriers by saying 'I will NOT be defined by my past, I will NOT allow these barriers to stop me doing what I want to do. I WILL overcome and become everything I want to be. Remember, the power of your words.

Do not allow past hurts, disappointments or tragedy stop you

Get up from where you are at. No one said it would be easy. In life, you have to keep on moving forward and stay focused. You have the power to break through those barriers-

You can get that dream job.

You can overcome those obstacles.

KEY 8
YOU CAN!!

But are you willing to break barriers and break those mindsets and go where you have always dreamed of going? The past cannot be changed. But the future is yet in your power.

Boldly going where you have never gone before!

KEY 9
THANKFUL.

I'm thankful for so many things. There is always something to be thankful for.

Are you feeling negative and can't seem to see the light at the end of the tunnel? When pessimistic thoughts enter your mind, just say, 'Thank God I'm alive.'

Today, focus on what you have and not what you don't have. You will realise you have more than you thought. More to be thankful for. Isn't that a great feeling?

Make it a daily habit to keep focused and have positive thoughts. When you do this, your mood will improve, and your life will feel more enriched. You will begin to have a different outlook on life and notice what is important to you. Ask someone today, "What are you thankful for?" If someone is speaking in a negative way, stop them in their tracks and ask them, "What are you thankful for?" They wouldn't be expecting that response. It will make them stop and think.

I came across this quote, and I thought I would share it with you.

'It's not happy people who are thankful
It's thankful people who are happy'- Unknown

What are you thankful for today?

KEY 10
POSITIVITY

I love Mondays!

1. Fresh start

2. The chance to set the tone for the rest of the week.

3. A great day to be alive.

Don't go rolling out of bed with that dreary look on your face thinking, 'Oh no, is it that time already?' Then start thinking about all the things you are dreading throughout the day. All the things you haven't completed. The things you need to accomplish today. The 'To Do list', which you haven't started. The list goes on and on. **STOP!**

You need to have a positive outlook.

It's a brand-new day so have positive thoughts! This will set the mood for the rest of your day.

'I am deciding to be positive and have positive thoughts.'

Whatever you are doing today **'positive vibes only.'**

I'll leave you with one of my favourite phrases:

'Wake up with **DETERMINATION**.

Go to bed with **SATISFACTION**'- Unknown

You did **NOT** wake up to be **MEDIOCRE**!

So, wherever you are, whatever you're doing, remember to have a positive mental attitude. It will take you further than you expect.

KEY 11
RESILIENCE IN THE FACE OF ADVERSITY

- **I CAN,** and **I WILL** overcome the challenges that present itself.

'My son was brutally murdered.'

'My sixteen-year-old daughter passed away in the night. We were preparing for her to come home the next day.'

"This is my third miscarriage. For years we have been longing for a child.'

'You won't see me for a while. I'll explain it all when I come back' (She didn't return. I later found out she was a victim of abuse).

I have been told many stories over the years of adversity. These are some of the unfortunate events that people found themselves in.

BUT, they all overcame the adversity. **HOW?**

I will share with you **4 KEYS** to overcoming. This will unlock the pain and set you free. You **CAN** overcome.

1. Have a support system around you to help and encourage you.
2. Have a positive mindset, knowing that things **WILL** turn around and get better.

3. Do **NOT** give up, stay strong and rise every time you fall.
4. Persevere, push past the pain, hurt and disappointment. Have that fighting spirit.

You **WILL** overcome.

Are you **WINNING**?

Give your best in everything you do.

YES, it will get difficult.

YES, you will feel pain.

YES, you will feel like giving up.

When you get to THAT point is when you **PUSH** that little bit harder, persevere and pursue your goals.

'When everything seems to be going against you, remember an aeroplane takes off against the wind' - Henry Ford

You are on the **WINNING** side.

Encourage someone today and tell them it is **WINNING** Wednesday. (If it IS Wednesday!!)

KEY 12
PROCESS IS THE KEY TO LIVING A FULFILLED LIFE

I **CAN'T** do THAT!

I **WON'T** do THAT!

Maybe I **WILL**. **NO, I WON'T**!

'I want to stay in the background, so that nobody will notice me. I do **NOT** want to be seen.'

FEAR! But what was I afraid of? My past, it haunted me. You cannot live in fear. 'I feel like a prisoner trapped behind prison bars. I have to break free, but how?'

Someone once said to me that fear is
False **E**vidence **A**ppearing **R**eal.

"Wow, that's deep", I thought.

KEY 13
PROCESS PROCESS PROCESS

That word keeps going through my mind. What does it mean?

The process is a series of actions or steps taken in order to achieve a particular end. (Oxford Dictionary)

OK- I have to get rid of the FEAR. Fear was stopping me achieving what I wanted to do. I was scared of failing; scared to be recognised. I had to take one step at a time. I had to take action. I had to go through a **PROCESS**.

Are you someone who experiences fear?

Have you overcome fear?

What steps did you take?

Please feel free to share what action you took. Your action may free someone else who feels that they are locked in a prison. Free someone today.

Fear has two meanings:

Forget **E**verything **A**nd **R**un

OR

Face **E**verything **A**nd **R**ise- Zig Ziglar

KEY 14
Motivation

There is a very inspiring and motivational talk by Maysoon Zayid (2014) entitled 'I Got 99 Problems... Palsy Is Just One'. She tells her extraordinary story of living with Cerebral Palsy. She talks about overcoming and not allowing people to stop you from achieving your goals.

There are many challenges in life that we will face, but it is how we deal with them that counts.

As you go through your day, think about how you will tackle the difficult situations you may find yourself in.

Here are **three** keys to tackling your problems.

1. **Avoid dwelling on your issues.**

2. **Focus on what is going right.**

3. **Help others.**

"You are a **WARRIOR**, not a **WORRIER**."
- James Victore

Breaking barriers

Do not let your circumstances be a barrier to prevent you from overcoming the challenges you may find yourself in.

I was teaching some students about potential barriers that you may face in life. They came up with some fantastic examples, I will just list a few:

- The past
- Life in general
- Circumstances
- Environment

Do any of these sound familiar? Barriers can prevent you from unleashing your potential. They can become a stumbling block and distort your vision, ultimately becoming a distraction. You can either do one of two things.

- You can allow the barriers to block your future, and then you become stagnant. You will then become ineffective and feel that your life has no purpose.

OR

- you can overcome the barriers by saying, 'I will **NOT** be defined by my past'. 'I will **NOT** allow these barriers to stop me doing what I want to do'. 'I **WILL** overcome and become everything I want to be'.

Remember the power of your words.

Do not allow past hurts, disappointments or tragedy stop you from shining like the star you are!

Do you want to know the truth about how to break those barriers? I will share with you a few tips that helped me break those barriers.

- It all starts with **YOU**. You have to believe in yourself. Have a clear mind, focus on your goals.
- What is it that you want to achieve? Focus on that particular thing.
- Keep moving forward and stay focused. Only **YOU** have the power to break through those barriers.
- Make one small change each day.
- Have a positive mental attitude.
- Always complete your goals- this will give you a sense of achievement.
- Say to yourself, **I CAN!!**

Be willing to break barriers and break those mindsets and go where you have always dreamed of going. The past cannot be changed. But the future is yet in your power. Boldly going where you have never gone before!

KEY 15
THE POWER OF YOUR RESPONSE

I was asked to speak at a women's event recently. I quickly answered "YES" I can do that. The event organiser was so excited that I responded positively. I am the sort of person that usually ponders and must think deeply before I respond with a 'NO'. However, I have decided I am changing the way I respond to situations.

I remember when I met my brother for the first time. It was the summer of 2016 to be exact, and I had recently turned forty. I actually felt that something super exciting was going happen that year as I reached the grand age of forty! I never in my wildest dreams thought that I would discover I had a brother!

I was an only child for my mum and wasn't raised with my dad.

When I was asked if I wanted to meet my brother, I responded with a YES very quickly! I didn't want to think about it as I may change my mind (I was good at that). I wasn't going to allow my past to define my response.

This was a door I chose to walk through; a door from my past. I knew the door wasn't closed, it was just that I had decided to carry on with my life. There came a point in my life where I faced the negative and decided to view things differently. That was when I knew that things were going to change because I decided to change. Things happen for a reason, but as you are going through it, you don't view it that way.

When we met, we both bonded immediately. Obviously, we had so much to share with each other. I'm glad I responded in a positive way because we get on so well and now have a beautiful relationship. If I had closed the door to my past, I wouldn't have been open to meeting my little brother. He is 3 years younger, he loves to call me the 'ELDER' sister. We now have the rest of our lives to get to get to know each other, and that is such a beautiful thing.

So, as you go through your day, remember the power of your response can change your direction.

KEY 16
TRANSFORMATION

If I was, to sum up, the word **Transformation** in two words, it would simply be **PERMANENT CHANGE.**

Have you ever thought about the way you speak to others? Your children, colleagues, strangers; the list goes on and on. Do you speak to them in a negative way?

Have you ever thought about the way you speak to yourself?

I'm so stupid...
I'm useless...
I'm...
I'm...

When we choose to speak in that way, it can have a negative impact on ourselves and others.

Transform the way you speak. Transform the way you respond to people and situations.

I'm sure you've heard that saying, *think before you speak.*

Transformation is a powerful word.

It speaks about making that permanent change.

Each day, decide to make a transformation in one particular area. It could be your speech, conduct, behaviour or responses. It could be anything in where you want to see lasting improvements.

Transform the way you think, speak and act. Make a decision today to make a transformational change!

KEY 17
RANDOM ACTS OF KINDNESS

Today, go ahead and make someone's day!

Yesterday, my boss and I were waiting to go into a Higher Education board meeting. For us, it was interesting although we had to confirm the learner's grades for the last semester/term. We were waiting for quite a while because another department was finalising their learner's grades.

So, we decided to go and grab a bite to eat while we were waiting. The soup looked inviting so I poured myself some. My boss agreed that it looked tasty! So, I went ahead and purchased my bosses' lunch too. He was so surprised, and he thanked me for his lunch. It was a small act of kindness, but it put a smile on his face.

What random act of kindness will you do today? Go ahead and put a smile on someone's face and make their day!

KEY 18
RADIATE POSITIVITY

I woke up today feeling inspired. It's Monday morning, and I am getting ready for the day ahead. I have a great big smile on my face, a bounce in my step. Today is going to be a **GOOD** day.

Positive mental attitude.

What are you facing today? Remember it is about your attitude towards the things you are going to face.

Do **NOT** roll over in bed and grab that duvet.

Do **NOT** press snooze.

Do **NOT** say 'I hate Monday's.'

Get **UP**, get **READY** and **GO** for it!

Have a positive attitude in everything you do.

Have a plan for the rest of your day.

If it's not working, change the method, but **DO NOT** change the goals.

I love playing Scrabble; I receive a 'Word of the Day' every day on my phone.

So, a word for the day is **POSITIVITY.**

Remember there is **POWER** in **POSITIVITY**.

Those are just a few keys that will help you on your journey. You are free; free to be you.

Go ahead and chase those dreams; walk through that door of opportunity! Embrace what lies ahead! I know it can be scary, but that's how you feel when there is going to be a change. Take that BOLD step then take one day at a time. You will be glad that you did!

THIS IS MY DECLARATION: -

I will **PURSUE** excellence in everything I do.
I will be **UNDEFEATED** and fight, I am a CHAMPION.
I will **STAY FOCUSED** and block out every distraction.
I will **HOLD** on and grasp tightly.
I will advance and move forward.
I will not allow the negative to overcast my mind.
I will stay positive.
I will not give up.
I will not quit.

Make a **DECLARATION** today. Despite what you are going through. The hardship, the disappointment, the hurt and the pain, or whatever it is that may come your way.

PUSH!

Pursue. Undefeated. Stay focused. Hold on!

DATE: _____

SIGNED: _____

About the Author
Tarnya Coley

Lecturer, Author and Motivational Speaker

A speaker who seeks to inspire, motivate, empower and create awareness to reach your full potential.

She is a firm believer in encouraging clients to be the best version of themselves, so they can become everything they set out to do.

Her desire is to help clients to understand the keys to living a pleasant and fulfilled life. Also exhibiting how they can make those small changes so they can achieve a better quality of life.

It is important to believe in yourself, because that is where it all starts!

OPEN DOORS

i Believe i Can

Enquiries & Bookings:

To enquire about booking Tarnya Coley to speak at your organisation, church or conference please see the information below.

My details:

Email: tarnya@ibelieveican.co.uk
Website: www.ibelieveican.co.uk

You can also find me on Facebook, Instagram, LinkedIn and Twitter

Publishers Afterword

Awesome Tarnya

Open Doors, I Believe I Can

I congratulate you on following your calling, your book and your journey to produce the book in such a short space of time is nothing less than miraculous.

I am blessed to meet you and publish your story,

May you continue to be a blessing, let your light shine.

Marcia M Spence

Published by Marcia M Publishing House

MARCIA M
PUBLISHING HOUSE

www.marciampublishing.com

Printed in Poland
by Amazon Fulfillment
Poland Sp. z o.o., Wrocław